The True Sto~~ry~~

The

Crows

In My

Garden

Based on Notes & Observations

Over 35 Short Stories Included

By Brian Weston & Keith Weston

The Crows In My Garden

Visit us at our website for more information:

Website: *thecrowsinmygarden.com*

Email: *thecrowsinmygarden@gmail.com*

Author & Co-Editor: Brian Weston
Co-Author & Editor: Keith Weston
Formatting & Design: Keith Weston
Proofreading: Tara McCormick, Ray Saunders, David Boyle, Joanne Weston

Publisher: Keith Weston
Paperback Published: January 6 2021
Nova Scotia, Canada
Word Count: 25,909
Paperback ISBN: 979-8-5889-6276-6

The Crows In My Garden

Quotes

"In all things of nature,
there is something of the marvellous."
- Aristotle

"Look deep into nature,
and then you will understand everything better."
- Albert Einstein

"Nature does not hurry,
yet everything is accomplished."
- Lao Tzu

Table of Contents

Chapter Three:

The Prince Of Crows

Chapter Four:

Magic In The Heir

Beyond The Chapters

Forward Entrance

This book is based on a true story, covering my experiences of interacting with and observing the wild crows in my garden. It has been reconstructed into a short story format, from the notes I made at the time and recalling events that transpired. I focused on the action that took place in each season, covering the years 2014, 2015, and 2016.

It began as a simple act of offering food to a seemingly hungry solitary crow, that led to an amazing adventure into the world of those clever black birds which are literally everywhere in Nova Scotia.

I have endeavoured to provide some insight into the structure of the crows hierarchy, social systems and feeding habits. Including offering some perspective on the seemingly *mundane fundamental activities of a crow family's daily life, with its distinct characteristics about their general and personal behaviours towards us and each other.*

So, if you are wondering by now - what some of your crows were doing or why they do the things crows do, then welcome to the world of our common garden crow.

A Garden Crow

I know not his ancestry
Nor any of his past,
And as for his intentions
I know just not to ask,

His origin's unknown to me
I've never seen his lair,
Of you or I or others
He just seems not to care,

A raucous call for cavalry
Single caws by three,
To tend the need of food again
It's all that he can see,

His daring moves and actions
Not relative or slow,
He is our friend and enemy
That common garden crow.

- Brian Weston

3

Chapter One

Genesis

Enter the crow,
A black silhouette,
That we all know..

Location, Location, Location

From September to December 2014

My observation point is from a second floor apartment, in a two storey house located in an older subdivision in Dartmouth, Nova Scotia, Canada.

I am positioned on top of a hill with my back kitchen door facing due south with the promise of all day sunshine. Stepping out on to my wooden balcony with a tremendous view of the surrounding area, I can see Lake Banook and Lake Micmac in the far off distance.

From my balcony I encompass about a 200 degree radius of sight, where I can easily see my own back garden as well as the backyards to my left and my right.

When I arrived, the lawn was well kept but the garden was in a wild state. Red roses lined the back edge of the house, with a variety of seasonal plants around the edge of the lawn, including a group a beautiful white orchids.

There are numerous types of trees inhabiting the area here including Red, Silver, Copper and Sugar Maples, with an assortment of Birch and Evergreens mixed in - forming a small sanctuary for wildlife.

The different colors of autumn display a sea of leaves ranging from spectacular cherry reds and fiery oranges with brilliant sunflower *yellows and gold in between, creating an absolutely breathtaking scene in the fall. It is truly magnificent to behold.*

There are lawns on the front and back of most houses in the surrounding neighbourhood. There is also a detached garage roof about 12 to 14 feet away from the balcony.

I wasn't aware at this time, that the lady next door to my left has five cats. There is also a stray cat in the immediate area, although at this point I had not seen any evidence of it yet, nor had I been looking.

The First Crow

Mid September

Meat & Greet

The day arrived for me to move in. I was not expecting any company and the last thought on my mind were crows.

I had just pulled in the driveway after getting home from the grocery store. I was still unpacking and trying to settle in, with stuff everywhere. As I was climbing the stairs to my apartment, I met my first crow. Sitting on the edge of the railing, the sun was shining brightly behind it as I came around the corner of the house, almost creating a silhouette in the contrast.

It seemed quite large. At first I thought it may have been a Raven. A male I presumed,

9

due to his size. His coat was jet black. I tried to speak to him saying *"Hello Crow"*. Without making a sound or any fuss, he sprang into the air and floated down landing gracefully on a tree branch overhanging the garage roof. At a little higher elevation to where I was standing on my balcony, we could clearly see each other.

After getting all of my bags and boxes inside, I noticed that he was still there. I had some left-over, grass-fed t-bone steak in my fridge which still had a bit of meat on it near the top. I put it, and some accompanying scraps out on the balcony railing.

He didn't seem to need any encouragement. I turned around to come back in and he was already headed for the balcony. Before I had the door completely closed behind me, he landed on the railing, ready to grab his spoils.

Eagerly and precisely, picking up each morsel, he managed to cram every bit in his beak; then he quickly tilted his head completely sideways to grab the whole t-bone as well! Taking a final glance at me while looking through the kitchen door window; possibly it was his way of saying thank you, before taking off.

Fully Loaded

"*Caaaw Caaaw Caaaw*" -

Three loud rapid caws got my attention. Calling from the balcony, my visitor announced his return late morning on the following day. I put some unshelled, unsalted peanuts that I had picked up for myself, out for him across the balcony railing.

I was watching him carefully pick up each piece and throw it to the back of his throat. I think he was watching me just as intently as I was watching him, never once taking his eyes off of me.

After eating a few he started to load up for later. His beak looked like peas all lined up in a pod. Not having any more room, he said thank you and headed out.

Jumping Jack

Showing up at around the same time every day, now more comfortable than ever. I noticed a distinguishing feature about him, which was never repeated by any of the other crows I encountered.

He preferred to land on the railing somewhere and when he got to the bend in the railing, he would jump over the corner gap and head right up to the window frame. I called him Jack, Jumping Jack.

One morning I caught him looking right into the kitchen window up close, peering inside.

Sometimes he would honk his arrival and sometimes not.

A friend of mine from Cape Breton told me that if I just left the door open he would come right inside my kitchen.

Invitation Only

After a few days, he must have felt very comfortable with all of this because he decided to bring a friend. Now there were two of them.

The second crow I guessed as being a female and maybe his best friend. It was slightly smaller and not so forthcoming, being more careful. She was hesitant until the door had been closed behind me. Only when a definite audible click shut was unmistakably heard would she come down for some food.

This became a standard behaviour with every female encounter. As I observed, they all displayed some extra caution and waited for the sound of the door closing before landing on the railing. Whereas the males would just fly right up.

The Menu

I started giving them any meat scraps I would normally have thrown out. They particularly seemed to like anything meat related raw or cooked. I occasionally bought a pack of chicken pieces on sale, these were usually inexpensive, lasting several days.

They couldn't resist peanuts in or out of the shell. Peanut butter applied to a piece of crusty bread worked wonders and appeared to slow their pace a little as they enjoyed savouring the taste.

Except for some ground beef with pasta sauce they did not want, these two crows would eat almost anything I offered them. I had heard from a friend that crows like chocolate but was a harmful addition to their diet as it can apparently affect their timing and interferes with their navigational equipment.

They loved fruit cake. I watched one morning after I gave out my last piece to Jack. He took his time picking out each piece of fruit, appearing to be savouring every one; then he gobbled the rest of the cake down. Jack flew into a tree near my position and it was as if he was tasting something with his tongue, just like you or I would.

Liver was their favourite by far with any other meats scoring as the next on their list of desirables.

There were no crows to be seen early in the day. Perhaps they had all gone to get some restaurant leftovers for breakfast or something. They all go somewhere first every day. Then show up here anytime from mid morning onwards until dark.

The Glove Experiment

October

I had a vision of him landing on my arm, or him eating his treats right out of the palm of my hand at some point in the future. I really had no idea of what to expect. I thought it would be ideal to wait for a less windy day to try something.

As it got colder, I noticed Jack couldn't wait for me to put the food down on the railing, hardly moving away from me at all. Consequently, I did not have to call him to me.

On the next windless day, I started to put his treats out wearing a garden type leather glove, he didn't seem to mind. I thought he might feel safer seeing and landing on a glove or something to cover my bare hand from his view.

The following day, still wearing the glove I walked out onto the deck and turned to face my kitchen door, standing there with my back against the railing. With my gloved hand I held a piece of roast chicken in my leathery fingertips as I gestured towards the waiting crow. In full view I didn't have to wait at all, Jack bounced along the railing right up to my glove. A quick look down to the left as he grabbed the chicken, another certain look towards me, possibly realizing that was a first for him too, then he pushed off the railing into the wind.

Whatever treats I put out for her, he would immediately come back and take that as well. Jack appeared to be flying away, but he was circling back, up onto the main roof of the building, waiting. I didn't understand why he would do this. I obviously had a lot to learn. I had to wait for him to get full before he let his companion have any.

I decided it was time for the next step. Later on that afternoon, I went out again with the glove on my hand and placed a treat on the centre of the palm. Again, he had no problem, approaching with a bounce in his step. Without hesitation, he used his beak to take it right from my palm. Then a brief glance at me with a tilted head before hopping off the rail into the wind.

He seems to have reached a level of trust with me and is comfortable with the whole process.

A Pair Of Jacks

November

"Kaaw, Kaaw" -

A new crow showed up one sunny and cold morning, this one had a sharper sounding caw to it. Watching from inside my screen door, I spotted him in a tree similar to the first one. I suspected it was a male because of its behaviour, fearless, cocky, and audacious to boot.

He was watching the first crow, Jack, bouncing along the railing, hopping over the corner gap to get to the food. **"Jack be nimble, Jack be quick."** After Jack had left, it wasn't long before he swooped in, taking the female crow's food.

It was just as daring, and hungry as Jack, although seemingly didn't care about their pecking order. Yet this third crow did wait for Jack to get his fill first before moving into position. I didn't know if they were related at this point. Probably being brothers, he would be just behind in line to the first one. I now had three crows showing up on a regular basis. Each with their own individual characteristics and related behaviours.

I wanted to let the new crow get acquainted with the proceedings, not that he was particularly interested in waiting for anything.

I embarked with the same experiment with the same glove I was using with Jack on this new male crow. Lured by a piece of pork chop, still producing identical results. Again I had visions of them eating right out of my bare hand at some point or maybe even perching on my arm.

It was getting noticeably colder. The new crow and female crow were watching Jack happily taking food from my gloved hand. I always kept any movements in mind as I didn't want to spook him, and I kept my hand just low enough so he didn't have to reach up high or anything like that.

The female however, was much more wary. She wouldn't even come down if I was standing inside the screen door with the glove on. Usually she responded to the door clicking shut, then came down from the tree. Even though I made sure not to make any sudden movements, the female was just not happy about the glove so I just put her food on the railing and came inside. I certainly didn't want to alienate them or jeopardize the situation in any way. I decided to discontinue any further experiments with the glove.

It has occurred to me that a crow although still always on alert, does develop a trust between himself and who they are encountering at the time. Acts of kindness especially involving food are noted even more. I wondered how do they communicate that level of trust regarding a particular person to each other?

Missing In Action

December

The morning became chilly as a breeze rolled in, with an overcast sky producing a dark scene, and light snow forecast for the majority of the day. Jack should have been here by now, but is no where in sight.

He'd been coming here for over two months now, arriving every day around late morning, usually before lunch time. For some unknown reason he was late that day.

I prepared his favourite - strips of raw beef liver, but he was missing in action. His friends were getting the treats instead. The sun was setting and I still hadn't seen him yet. I had an awkward feeling that all was not well.

I went out onto my balcony and tried calling him, *"Jack! ... Jack!"* and knocking the railing with a fork which I sometimes did by accident. There was of course, no response. I even asked the remaining crows if they'd seen him?

During the first week of December, just as suddenly as he first appeared, it became clear that Jack had vanished and I never saw him again.

He had great character and demonstrated so much potential. It was a loss from my perspective. I was disappointed to say the least. The other crows appeared a bit upset but they couldn't tell me where he was. I have no clue what happened to him. I suspected an untimely end by some means.

Since Jack was the only crow that ever did the corner jump thing, I knew I'd recognize him again just from that. Occasionally a crow would land on the railing nearest my window and not travel the corner, just to take a peek into my kitchen, It was never Jack.

Getting To Know Mr. Crow

December

It was down to two crows again, but not for long. It's getting close to our holiday season so I knew I'd have all kinds of treats for them. I wasn't quite sure yet what I was getting myself into.

"Honk Honk!!" -

Aha, here he is wanting to know why I hadn't noticed him earlier, and was making him wait. *"Just a moment Mister Crow"*, I said to him as I went to the fridge just inside my kitchen door and pulled out a blue food container. I kept their collected treats in one place. I do believe they came to recognize it through the window, *"Yup, he's getting the food ready"*.

This new dominant male was as brazen as the first one. He'd circle back and take anyones food. It didn't seem to matter who you were, he was first. If he was full he'd still come back to get more if he needed it or not. The others never ever got in his way.

Whenever I went outside there was always a crow or two around. Mr. Crow was consistently close by, ready to just drop in anytime. After I'd been out, it was never long before I could hear his distinct *"Caw, caw caw"*, coming from the railing outside.

One particular time he swooped in and took what I had just put out for someone else. He took off towards the front of the house, where was he going with all that food? I hurried to my living room window and watched him land in my front garden area. I watched in disbelief as he proceeded to quickly bury all the food he had just taken. Then took up position somewhere on the roof again out of my sight. He was getting ready to swoop in for more as soon as I had put it out.

There was a notable incident quite late in the day when it was almost dark. I was surprised to see the crows still around my place at this time of day. Mister had left the perch and circled back after leaving with his mouth quite full. Attempting to land again this time on the railing nearest my stairs. I tried to shoo him away by blocking him from completing his task, allowing the others to get some.

He dropped most of the contents he had just collected from his beak as he exuded a very loud *"KKKAAAWWW!"*. Executing a sudden change of direction with his claws out, he was already anticipating clutching the railing.

As if to say *"HEY C'MON YOU'RE NOT ALLOWED TO DO THAT - NOT TO ME"*.

Mr. Crow seemed greatly offended that I did this as if I had humiliated him in front of the others. This was not my intention. He didn't like it one bit.

I immediately apologized and backed away offering him the whole end of the railing to himself. All the other crows had retreated, it was just the two of us, and the fresh beef liver waiting to be devoured.

Looking a little shaken as he re-landed and flicked his feathers, making a few clicks as he did so. Was he thinking *"Hmm that's more like it"* while he looked all around?

As he visibly pulled himself back together and had gathered his bearings he went straight for the goods. After a fast reload he took off, and was gone for the night.

I had tried putting food in different places on the railing and the other crows were okay with it but he came first. I resigned myself to this but didn't understand the situation. I thought Mr. Crow may be a relative (i.e. son) of a higher up. I assumed he held some kind of rank or position. At this point in time, I knew relatively little about crow hierarchy. I started to wonder what territory they occupied and what their families consisted of.

Meeting The Elders

Late December, January

One afternoon, right before the New Year just as it was getting dark, two more crows appeared. These were a little larger than any others I had encountered so far. Gracefully and quietly landing over by the furthest part of the corner railing at the top of my stairs. I guessed that they had maybe been watching from a distance, just observing. My interest in them was growing.

A regal pair. Like two soldier's helmets from the guards at Buckingham Palace standing side by side; being calm and mature, like elder crows or something. I estimate that these crows held some kind of rank or maybe being more of an Elder's Council that's come to check out what they've heard so much about. These elders were

35

more patient, not in a hurry for food; never bouncing around or anything like that. Completely unfazed by anything, very stoic. Just an occasional blink. Letting the younger male do his thing first and then the females next. Watching.

After coming inside and it had quieted down, they both sauntered over one behind the other. Not in a hurry, with a serene composure they took some treats before taking off. I noticed again what appeared to be a definitive effort of thanks from them, or acknowledgement; by holding your gaze and/or eye contact with their prize in-beak before takeoff.

Who were these visitors? They certainly were not your average crow by any assessment. The reason for honouring us with their presence today, will remain a mystery. I was expecting Mr. Piglet to come swooping down to take the food but he didn't. Watching from a safe distance and intentionally not interfering out of respect. I wondered what an Elder was? Rank, position, or birthright. What about age and experience? How would they qualify?

Chapter Two

Bring On Spring

Glimpse into the world of crows,
The dark knights of the winter snows..

Know Snow

From February to May 2015

This fall and the beginning of this winter has been an eye opener. I have witnessed some different scenarios that exhibited significant crow behaviours. The characters I had encountered so far, some of which were destined to be with me for a little longer, were displaying an intelligence which I had not really anticipated, nor had I observed in any other animal. I was about to discover a lot more as our first spring together was around the corner and about to transpire before my very eyes. There was never a dull moment.

The crows have had a rough winter, as well as all the other birds and animals that have been outside. All having to survive these extra winter storms that they would not normally have to contend with. It's causing them to be a bit confused. The trees are certainly hesitant. Wildlife of all types must be running low on their saved up food reserves or completely out by now.

Recently, the local radio stations have been asking the public to remember the birds and the squirrels during this late spring. They were encouraging responsible feeding where and if possible.

The crows had hardly seen my car during the winter, and nor had I for that matter. We had so much snow from all the Nor'easters that there wasn't any point in having to keep digging my car out every few days. There was nowhere for the snow to go. I left the car parked off to the side in the driveway and worked around it.

The snow persisted, dumping over 109 inches during February and March. The temperatures were well below the seasonal average and delayed any melting or thawing. The daily combinations of wind and sleet didn't help conditions and early April was surprisingly cold, wet and miserable with snow still on the ground.

An Injured Crow

Early February

First thing I noticed as I looked outside this morning was how cold it looked. There is a layer of light snow covering everything. It was minus 12 Celsius with a frozen fog drifting through the garden, and I could see brief rays of sun shining through the overcast sky.

Wearing a lightweight jacket I had just stepped outside, and **"OH!"** I instantly felt the brisk wind through the material. It felt a lot colder than it was. I was putting some treats on the railing when a male crow attempted to land on it from my left. His right foot was clenched in a ball and was obviously useless.

I could see the anguish in his face, beak opened in a painful grimace, ***"Scraawwww, scwar caaw Caww"***. The need for food had brought him here but he couldn't complete a landing. I couldn't determine what was actually wrong with his foot. Who was it I wondered, it wasn't Mr. Crow.

With the momentum he was carrying, he slid along the railing until he fell off landing on the garage roof. It was hard enough to navigate with two good feet let alone just one. This put him in immediate danger. Having the use of both feet is imperative to him making it through the rest of the winter.

I could see his distress. He looked afraid. I told him not to worry and that I will always feed him. All he needed to do was to show up, which thankfully, he did; preferring to arrive just a little after the rush hour so he could take his time getting to the food. Whenever he came around I fed him all he could eat.

This guy stayed on the garage roof as I threw his food right to where he was. Unable to chase any scraps that made it near him, the food would end up rolling off the roof. He'd only fly off when he had enough and always seemed very grateful.

Visiting often, his foot showed some improvement as soon as the temperatures had risen above zero. As he got better he still had a limp, just like we would have, but I couldn't give him a walking stick. Fortunately for him, he must have healed the ailing parts. His pronounced limp disappeared with the onset of spring and he blended back into a relatively normal crow life with his friends and relatives.

As far as I could tell, this crow did not have any distinguishing features about him, he was like an average Joe crow. I was not able to tell him apart from the other crows from this point on.

The Stray Cat

February

Today as I looked out of my front window I couldn't help but notice a set of undisturbed paw prints on the fresh snow from early this morning. I looked around but there was no one about. The tracks went into my neighbours yard to the left. There was no way I could tell the tracks apart with five more cats prints all over the place.

It snowed again that night. Enough to identify more fresh paw prints coming right up my stairs to the railing. It looked like it had sniffed about a bit then made its way back down my staircase and across the road to the other side of the street. Again, there were no cats in my yard now, but it could still be around here somewhere.

It was showing minus 12 Celsius outside on my thermometer, with almost no wind to speak of. It was just before dusk as I went out on to my balcony for some fresh air, the crisp winter scent marked the height of the season. I was looking out and downward over my snow covered front lawn. There at the end of my driveway, camouflaged between chunks of snow from the snowplough was a white cat; I say white but he did have some black splashed over him.

He was crossing over to the other side of my street. He looked pretty bedraggled and uncared for. He was definitely not one of the five from next door. This was the stray cat. Four crows came out of nowhere and immediately began scolding him. *"Caww, Caww, Kaww, Kaww"*, blared from the treetops. He was leaving anyway and quickly slipped out of sight through a space in the fence.

The lady next door had told me a little about him. She said that he just shows up now and again, but doesn't bother her cats any.

To me he seems to be the four legged higher plains drifter type, likely an un-neutered tom.

I didn't see him for a while but did see occasional tracks here and there. He must be able to smell the meat and comes around to investigate. The silence and stealth of this hungry cat made him difficult to observe. An instinctual survivor. With all of his experience outside he must be a natural born hunter. We referred to him as Hunter so often it became his name.

I hoped he had a home base somewhere close and warm during these Nor'easters. With nothing to protect his feet he's out there regardless searching for food.

Sky Diving Seagull

Early March

Late one morning I was standing outside my kitchen door. There was about eight inches of fresh snow on the ground. While clearing the snow away, a seagull just fell out of the sky right onto the balcony in front of me.

Being a young herring gull from this season, it still had mottled pre adult feathers. It had survived the winter thus far. Flapping about, I could see it wasn't able to stand. It had what appeared to be a dead rubber foot. As soon as it realized where it had landed, I heard a garbled squawk - ***"Sqwwauurrrk!"***. It frantically managed to flap its way up over the deck railing using a snow piled garden chair and somehow landed onto the garage roof.

Two other adult seagulls immediately attacked it by knocking it over repeatedly across the garage roof. It must have been just about done. I threw some food to it. Apart from the food sinking in the snow, it thought I was throwing food at it instead of to it. It was trying to evade the food. Unable to take off yet, it took another bump from behind from a single gull. It couldn't move any further.

It was exhausted and injured, probably starving as well. I came back out again and was able to throw some pieces of squashed up bread very near it. Now realizing I wasn't just throwing stuff at it, the hungry gull began to take the food. I was able to throw a couple of raw meatballs very close to it which were quickly gulped down.

When I came out later my guest was still there. In the same spot from when I last checked. I tossed some more bread in his direction and it stayed there for several hours. As dusk approached, I noticed the gull was gone. I was not really expecting to see it again but hoped for the best.

The seagull intrusion didn't seem to bother the crows. They didn't mind as long as their provisions were not being affected. The crows were never aggressive or defensive towards this injured seagull.

The next morning around 10:00 am I was out on my balcony talking to a couple of crows in the tree above the garage, when down onto the garage roof came the injured gull. Somehow it had survived the night and had remembered where I was, or more than likely, the place where it last got food. All the meatballs and bread combined probably was the equivalent to getting a hamburger, and it had come back for the fries.

It came back again and again, looking a little less fragile but still with a useless leg and foot. It was hopping on one leg and trying hard to get around. He earned the nickname Hoppy.

I continued feeding him and he slowly improved. He did his best to defend himself when attacked by the other gulls, and actually fought back sometimes. He gradually appeared to be getting stronger. Staying around until the late spring, still hopping about but looking much better, time will tell when he'll be able to rejoin his flock.

Garden Courtship

March

Despite the snow and it being very cold, the crows came every day. There were about eight to ten crows regularly visiting the garden. Throughout the winter at any given time, it was the same dominant male Mr. Crow and his immediate colleagues. Elder visits are becoming infrequent now, I haven't seen them since January, possibly like us the weather affects their travel plans.

There were a couple more that kept at the back of things. I thought them to also be females because of the additional caution they displayed. There were always the two of them who arrived close together. They would land on the same branch at the far right of the back garden very close to the garage roof.

I had just put some treats out on the railing for Mr. Crow and was going back inside as the two females swooped in to land in their tree. As I closed the door I saw only one crow on the branch. My first thought was *'Well there were two of them, now where's the other one?'.*

My view of that corner of the garden is obstructed when I am inside the house because of the balcony. I had to go to another room to the left of my kitchen to get a better view.

The missing, presumed female crow, was crouched low in the snow on the very edge of where the lawn ends. My first thoughts were that she was injured. Instead she took a posture with her wings about a third open on each side and her tail wagging back and forth. She was making a very strange calling sound, almost like a muffled tuba. That is when Mr. Crow swooped off the railing and made a spectacular open winged noisy entrance landing right in front of her in the fresh snow, *"Caaww!"*. Mr. Crow's head bowed and he puffed himself all up with his wings spread and his tail fanned out. He too was making a very non-crow sounding noise like a long extended muted honking, *"honnnnk"*. I was absolutely astonished. Watching a crow's mating dance right here, almost on the lawn. Mr. Crow proposing to Ms. Crow?

Or, had they perhaps known each other for some time, and had realized that this garden could be the right place, as well as the right time, to raise a family.

They both flew up into a maple tree near the back of the garage and sat there together, beaks touching. From my position I could see that Mr. Crow is grooming her. I thought to myself *'I'll put my binoculars away now and give them some privacy'.*

It must be a rare occurrence to see this so close to suburbia and right here in my garden. Without rings to express their commitment to each other, they have clearly established a bond that may last a lifetime.

I noticed that much of the same feeding pattern persisted, with Mr. Crow being very brave and Mrs. Crow remaining cautious. She flies up into the nearest tree when I come out and waits until I leave to retrieve her food.

I could see them during a sunny lunch hour, sitting together. I put out some raw ground beef for them. Mr. Crow flew onto the perch, looked back at Mrs. Crow and hopped 180 degrees to face her. Cawing a few times in her direction, she didn't move at all and didn't make a sound. He looked back at the ground beef then back at her. A moment later he turned around, grabbed his share of the beef and flew up over the house out of my sight. I came back inside and closed the door, then right away Mrs. Crow quietly came down, taking her half and following Mr. Crow toward the roof. It was as if he tried waiting for her to land before taking the food.

Nest Crafting

Late March to Mid April

I have noticed several crows have congregated in the garden, exploring around the base of the trees. They are not necessarily looking for food, just mulling about on or near the ground. I could hear their chattering, although without making a lot of noise. ***"Ca..Caw, c..ca, *click* c..caa"***. It seems like they are looking for something. Aha, I see one crow with a twig in its mouth, but drops it. He begins pulling on a bigger one. Another is doing the same thing, they must be considering building a nest. It seems way too cold and unsettled for that yet.

There are four crows in my garden. It's just about lunch time. It's dry and the sun is out but it is still very cold. They must know something I don't. Maybe they're all going to build a nest close by.

Today the crows are actually in the trees pulling on twigs and jumping around, looks like there's going to be two nests here somewhere with all the activity that's going on. I hope so, I can't wait to see baby crows around. I'll need to make a kind of table or platform for them to land on. I hope the weather gets sorted out in time.

"Like it or not, warm enough or not, we're building a nest, right in your garden. Not much cat activity, winter cats are inside and there couldn't be a closer food supply."
- (Imaginary voice of Mrs. Crow)

Yes, they are building a nest. Right in front of me, right in the middle of the trees next to the garage. I am going to be able to see the whole thing, it's very exciting, this is going to be so good. At first I didn't understand that there were four crows in the same immediate area though. It turns out that upon further investigation, there are two crows actually building the nest and the other two are helping. Two crows are bringing presumably good nest building twigs and sticks and the female (Mrs. Crow) is sorting through them and selecting which ones she wants. She is the head nest architect as well as the interior designer, with Mr. Crow helping her arrange materials in the tree. I wonder who the other crows are that are helping?

The nest is about 25 feet up in a Sugar Maple tree. It's fairly central, carefully wedged in a strong fork and is probably close to completion as Mrs. Crow is gathering some yellow grass from last season for the lining. It still seems a little too early yet as it is still cold and very windy. There's no protection from the elements by the tree itself. The helpers are still around but I think that their work is finished as Mrs. Crow is finishing off her nest by herself.

Mrs. Crow is sitting now and, presumably, is going to lay some eggs. I wondered how many eggs she has laid? I will be counting the days until they hatch. Helpers are gone now except for stopping in for a snack. Mr. Crow is around a lot, he doesn't seem to be doing any sitting himself but does guard the nest when Mrs. Crow takes off for some food and a wing stretch, she's never away for very long. Mr. Crow is never far away either and usually sits higher up somewhere close, especially at night.

I decided to go to the hardware store to buy some wood and other materials for a perch. The size I went with was approximately 12 x 18 inches x 3/4 inch thick. I have screwed this onto the railing with a set of right angle brackets, it feels quite sturdy. It's flush with the inside railing and protrudes out towards the garden. This provides a bit of a landing pad for them. I have also introduced a dish of clean water in case she needs a drink and doesn't want to travel far to get some.

It's been close to two weeks since Mrs. Crow started sitting, so I expect that something may be close to happening very soon. The weather has been awful, with blustery winds, cold temperatures and everything is wet. I am very surprised that Mrs. Crow is still with the task. She must be very hardy and is going to be a good mother to her chicks when they arrive.

Day 20

Today is the first time I have seen Mr. Crow bring food to the nest, I don't know if it's for her or the chicks. It must be hatching time given a day or two either way. It is Sunday and the weather forecast isn't good for this upcoming week.

Who's Prey

April

A few days ago right after I finished lunch, I put some chicken out on the railing for Mr. Crow, out of nowhere he squawked loudly and took off in a hurry from right in front of me.

It startled me briefly; following Mr. Crow, I leaned around the corner of the house towards the staircase and watched.

He shot upwards, squawking as he went -

"CAAAWWWAAAskaaww!"

It was an Osprey, circling as they do sometimes in the afternoons. I got out my binoculars and could see it coming in from the North, maybe on its way to the lakes.

Mr. Crow wasn't taking any chances. He hadn't stopped calling since he took off. An Osprey isn't to be taken lightly. Being smaller than an Eagle an Osprey is larger than any of the hawks and with its razor sharp extra-curved fish-holding talons it can inflict a destructive wound at any time.

The Osprey was directed off course by him initially and then harassed by a posse of cohorts. A group of admonishing crows was enough to deter it for now.

I have heard of there being Bald Eagles in the area but had not seen one yet. I don't think Mr. and Mrs. Crow have that much to worry about. Help arrives quickly and serves as a warning to other birds.

Mr. Crow and his cohorts are doing a great job defending, I wonder what else I've missed.

This is just what I have seen only by being on my balcony at the right time.

I expect these intruders will likely just move over a bit the next time they are passing through, it's not worth the bother to them. I am imagining our migrant Osprey visitors who are only here for the summer, are tending to a family of their own.

It is remarkable that Mr. Crow's calls for help were answered promptly. For this particular call must surely carry a level or sense of emergency, maybe via a code or an inflection applicable to the current situation, communicating its severity.

A Crow Funeral

Late April

On a Sunday

We received light winds and it stayed around minus 1 Celsius throughout the cloudy night. The day began with the passing clouds changing into an icy fog for the remainder of the morning. The sun was out, shining in the afternoon, raising the temperature but the wind had steadily increased.

It's been strange weather to say the least. The temperatures are so varied, the trees don't know if they should continue their pre spring awakening or wait a little longer.

Mrs. Crow has been faithfully sitting on her eggs, under the watchful eye of Mr. Crow. The upcoming weather wasn't sounding good, low temperatures and rain was forecast for the next few days. Both parents are already totally soaked through, and I suspect the nest must be as well. The nest is getting the full brunt of the weather.

There must be chicks in the nest because Mr. Crow is bringing food. After a few bits for himself Mr. Crow took a beak full of chopped liver up to the nest and a patient Mrs. Crow.

Something was going on in the nest. I kept my hopes up. I can't see into the nest from my vantage point due to the nest being slightly higher than my eye level. I hope the weather lets up for them some, as this isn't looking good.

Monday

It's still raining and blowing hard, and is just a few degrees above freezing. A heavy fog rolled in during a solid eight hours of snow followed by six hours of light rain at near zero degrees all day long.

The crows are still working hard. I've left a few strips of raw liver on the perch but they aren't as interested today. I think they are trying to keep the nest as warm as possible.

Tuesday

The temperature hovered around freezing for most of the day and rose slightly as the afternoon wore on. Weather for the day consisted of over five hours of snow and I could see more fog coming in after lunch, only to get over seven hours of rain as it got darker for the night.

To my surprise, Mrs. Crow was still sitting as it was snowing and raining again directly on her. Poor Mrs. Crow, she has to be a special crow to sit through this atrocious weather. There's no cover or protection for Mr. Crow either. Sitting close by to her demonstrating his unwavering support through it all.

The railing was cleaned off and I put some food out if they wanted any. As the door closed Mrs.Crow flew to the perch and was taking as much as she could but was doing so in panic mode, she couldn't wait to get back to the nest. Mr. Crow guarded from nestside when she was away, I could see him looking into the nest as Mrs. Crow arrived home.

My only view of them through the snow were of their backs as Mrs. Crow appeared to be feeding the chicks. Visibility wasn't great.

Mr. Crow eventually landed on the perch, he did seem agitated and upset. He ate some of the chopped kidney I had put out. I thought it would be easier to feed to the chicks. Then he took off somewhere but wasn't to the nest. It was going to be a long day for them.

The rain stopped for about an hour late afternoon just before dusk, and an even stronger wind persisted, but Mrs. Crow was still vigilant, she seemed determined to go the distance. I was impressed but really concerned. This was a super crow moment.

Wednesday

The temperature here was at zero all night with light winds. It was 1 degree Celsius when I got up at about 6:30 this morning. The sky was a thick overcast.

I can see the nest through my kitchen door window. It is cold and miserable. The first thing I noticed was that the nest was unattended. My heart sank.

Mrs. Crow, or Mr. Crow were nowhere to be found. Or, really any sign of a crow anywhere for that matter. I feared the worst and put a rain jacket on and went outside to have a look around.

Standing on my balcony, I looked over the garden. There wasn't a crow to be seen or heard anywhere, in any direction - which was a little strange because there are usually one or two around somewhere at any given time.

Later that morning I noticed there hadn't been any activity around the nest or anywhere for that matter, which was confirming my fears. I decided to go up the tree so that I could see for myself what was or wasn't going on.

At about 10:30 am, I got a pair of steps from the garage to get into the bottom of the tree. I began my ascent up toward the nest, which was far more difficult than I thought especially as it was drizzling and cold. My hands were freezing.

There were still no crows anywhere and the nest seemed higher than looking at it from my usually elevated position. When I reached the nest and looked inside I didn't see anything at all to begin with, it just looked as though the bottom of the nest had been roughed up and disturbed with nothing in it. I was expecting to see egg shells or something. Anyway, upon further investigation I found two tiny stone cold baby chicks with basically only their thin skins to protect themselves with. They felt like little blocks of ice they were so cold.

I was deeply saddened by my discovery. As being their Mum and Dad, they must have been devastated.

The nest was absolutely sodden and cold with pieces of ice within it. They didn't stand a chance. It appears that both parents had done their best to actually bury their chicks in one side of the nest then dug or scraped the rest of the floor of the nest over on top of them. I picked one up to take a closer look. They could be just a couple of days old, if that, and despite Mrs. Crow's best efforts to protect them from the elements, didn't stand much of a chance. Baby crows must not have a method for regulating their body temperature and rely solely on their mother for their warmth. The only protection offered by the tree itself were the tiny buds but nothing to break the wind or divert any rain.

As the chicks were already buried within it, I thought it best to cover them up, leaving them and the nest exactly as I had found them.

I could feel the cold air against my back and I could hear the sound of the wind rattling tree branches around me but I hadn't been paying attention to anything except navigating the tree. I did not notice the actual beginning of what was transpiring around me and on the block, which consists of four detached houses and their respective gardens and tree lines. I heard some noise which was definitely crows, looking up and around me I was surrounded. I saw dozens of them. I realized they were swooping and diving directly right at me in the tree. With over a hundred crows cawing, the noise was absolutely chaotic.

There were several crows flying right around the top of the tree, and circling the immediate tree area. Some of these were very close. The noise got louder as I descended to the ground. As I did, I looked up, there must have been 100 to 200 or more crows all flying around, calling out frantically to each other and at me. I had been caught red handed intruding on a site that obviously had great significance to them.

As I stepped away from the tree, looking up again and all around, five crows had landed in the tree next to the nesting tree above the garage. It appeared these five were all elders. Still squawking ferociously right at me, as were all the other crows. Some of which were still circling overhead, while many had landed in nearby trees. This was true surround sound.

I had a pretty good relationship with the parent crows and some of their immediate family because I had been feeding them on my balcony since September of the previous year. Crows have a way of identifying you, so you are either a good guy or a bad guy.

Amidst the commotion, my very first instinct was to move out in clear view, first - to the five crows above me. Motioning with open empty hands, I tried to make it as clear as possible that I had nothing in them, and I had not taken any young ones. I looked up to the top of the tree and said out loud:

**"I don't have your babies,
they are exactly where you left them."**

I pointed to the nest. I showed and waved my empty hands again. To my total astonishment the noise began to diminish and within less than a minute it ceased altogether. It went completely silent. Just for a moment. They all just sat there in the trees, on my neighbours right and along the property line, not a sound, as if it were their moment of silence. The five crows in the tree directly above me were having a real good look, when one squawked out an unusual crow call which I had not previously heard before, *"CAAWAAH!"*. I assumed it meant that they understood I hadn't done any harm. A decision must have been made because after the signal, one by one, the five elders took off in the direction of Lake Micmac. Then the others began to leave as well, singularly and in groups of twos and threes.

I was amazed at what happened, had I just witnessed *'A Crow Funeral'* of sorts? I wondered where all of these crows came from so quickly? Did a crow see me intruding? Was a distress call given? Or was I just in the wrong place at the wrong time?

I noticed that from this event onwards that crow activity went to a minimum. Hardly a visit to my balcony since this moment. Not one bird went near the tree, let alone the nest. It became very quiet, as if the area had been designated a *'No-fly zone'.*

I've heard in conversation over the years that a group of crows making a lot of noise and commotion are what's called *'A murder of crows'.* I had different ideas as to why they might do this over a dead crow. Could it be a mourning ritual of the loss of one of their own family. After witnessing my own tragic crow situation it has me leaning towards it being a funeral for their own.

I had my own moment of silence for them. As a symbol of my greatest condolences, I took a large stone from the rose section of the garden and etched the date into it; I then placed it at the base of the nesting tree, in recognition of their loss and to remember what took place here. It was a tragic day.

The Unforgotten Crows

All of them
And all they'll be,
Are all you'll ever
Or never see,

They did not wait
And hadn't rest,
Fell deep in love
Then built a nest,

This is it
Forlorn alas,
'Twas such a moment
That came to pass,

Rushing out
In wild despair,
So many crows
Had filled the air,

Their home built up high
Which now is torn,
From all the weather
This place we mourn,

Not one came
As far as can see,
No creature landed
In the nesting tree,

Knowing it's over
Their family is gone,
They had no choice
Their lives moved on,

It all fades away
In greens and in grace,
Perhaps another time
In a different place.

- Brian Weston, Keith Weston

Chapter Three

The Prince of Crows

Three lookouts perched,
"We saw that!",
Sound the alarm –
For an incoming cat!

A New Beginning

From September 2015 to January 2016

It was relatively quiet throughout the summer with very little activity. I think that the crows go further away from home and frequent farms for easy food. They start coming back into town for the fall. The lady next door had told me they'll be back if there's food available. **"They won't forget you"** she said.

There wasn't a crow to be seen all through August. They weren't interested in my balcony takeout menu. There was certainly never a crow in the nesting tree, none came near it. I didn't see a crow in that tree until late September. I wonder how they marked it out?

I have been here for one year now. I wondered if this summer was quiet because they go somewhere every summer or because of what happened here in the spring? I must admit, I really did enjoy having all the different crows around. They were fascinating company to have as my friends.

Was there ever a consideration of losing such a welcome food supply? Will there be a run back to the garden in the fall? **"We'd better claim this garden asap before someone else does."**

How will this next season unfold? Nearing the end of September I was given my first clue ...

New Crow'nd Prince

September

I decided to put the water dish out on the perch in case anyone needed a drink. Crow activity was minimal. September was coming to a close and I wondered how many crows if any, would end up here again during the winter.

No sooner than I had closed the door behind me, while turning around to face out, I saw a crow land on the railing to my right. He hopped over to the water dish and took a few sips while keeping a close eye on me. He seemed to savour the clean cold water. I just watched through the glass and wondered if he would come back again, and how would I recognize him?

I came back to my kitchen door with a piece of raw hamburger patty and showed it to him through the window. He looked at me and the burger, very intently. I cracked the door open slowly as not to alarm him but he flew into the closest tree anyway. I put the food on the perch, turned around and came inside. A few seconds after I closed the door, he came down and inspected the meat, then grabbed it in his mouth. He looked at me again, making eye contact before taking off.

I have come to believe this is their way of saying thanks for the food. I saw this replicated over and over and it was conducted by both males and females, they always turned to the door having a look again before taking off. They just seemed grateful that someone had taken the time and gave them something to eat.

I was assuming that this was indeed another male, he seemed kind of cocky and brazen. Out of every crow that landed on the perch, this one always kept an eye on what was going on under the perch on the ground, as well as an all around general awareness.

This guy came back later in the day. I noticed a small feather sticking up and out towards the back to the outside of his right wing. It was how I was able to easily recognize him as being the same crow that had been here before.

I didn't know it yet but this was to be the new Prince of Crows, at least in this garden. He came back two to three times a day for a treat. He moved to the end of the railing when I came outside holding the food out in front of me. I gently opened the door with my left hand and put the food down with my right. He bounced down the railing enthusiastically to take his reward, a thank-you, then liftoff. All with me standing right there.

Greeting Royalty

Late September

After a few more days, I went outside and tried saying hello to my new companion multiple times before I put the treat down. He'd hop to the left then back to the right. He looked at me intently, then wiped his beak back and forth a few times on the railing. It seems to be a gesture of comfortability.

The second time I did this I got a surprise. He landed on the railing then hopped onto the perch and flicked all his feathers. Puffing out his neck and kind of lowering his head, he made a sound sort of like low purring soft rattle *"prrrrt, prrrrt"*. He did this twice and then it was like, *"Ok, where's the food?"*. Incidentally, he hasn't actually honked hello yet, but he does repeat this behaviour often.

On the last day of September, looking through my screen door, I watched as he flew from my balcony railing into the forbidden tree of last season. Landing near the abandoned nest, he swayed up and down on a thinner branch just looking at it.

With a series of short jumps and some help from his wings he reached the top of the tree. While holding his wings open, he began to broadcast a sequence of loud caws - *"Caaw Caw Caw Caw Caaaaw!"*.

Maybe this was like an explorer settling in an ancient land, because later that day I noticed two crows perched in the tree together. This led me to believe his vocalizations and physical display in the tree signified to his friends it was now okay to return to this location. It was as though he had staked his claim to this garden and was moving in.

I continued seeing resemblances in this crow's behaviours that I had noticed in Mr. Crow from last season. He appeared to be everywhere or close by, all the time. He'd land right on the perch if I was outside, so close to me. Very trusting. He certainly had his spirit. It felt right to call him Spirit, whether Mr. Crow came back or not.

He was undoubtably first, and wasn't going to let anyone forget it. If he wasn't the first crow on the perch or railing he soon would be. Edging up beside another crow, he would unexpectedly kick or just push the other crow clean off. Never any fighting, just a reminder - *"This is my spot"*.

Chief Of Operations

October

In October of this season, in my infinite wisdom, I decided to get a cat. I thought it would be a good idea to adopt an indoor cat, a cat that had only been inside so far. I went to a local animal shelter and met a lovely character that I brought home, intending to give him a permanent spot to live. His name was Chief, a beautiful athletic eight year old Chocolate Point Siamese. He never had the free roam of being outside before, so I wasn't too concerned about him catching a bird or anything like that.

After I had gotten him home at about 5:30 pm he started howling, it was loud. ***"MRROOWW!"*** No matter how much consoling I offered, he was pretty stressed out. According to the shelter, Chief had apparently been used to a life of luxury and had belonged to a wealthy owner that passed away unexpectedly. He meowed, making the most incredible amount of noise. I had to wait it out.

I placed a blanket on one end of my couch for him to sleep in if he wanted to. *"Morrroww!!!"* is what he had to say about that.

I was hoping for a miracle as I turned out the lights to retire. To my complete astonishment it stopped, as soon as the light went out he became completely silent. Perhaps he was trying to tell me he wanted the light off all along.

The next morning, Chief seemed much more attuned to his new environment. He was not making the racket he was last night. He figured out the front view and the back but couldn't make up his mind which was best.

Intrigued by what was going on outside, he liked to sit on the window ledge and watch me feed the crows. I suppose Chief became my new supervisor. The crows weren't sure what to make of him. They had probably not seen a cat with these markings before, so a Siamese was still a cat (the enemy) to them. Although, he was far more interested in the starlings, which he could see from both the front of the house and the back.

That evening was totally different than the first. He was visibly more relaxed. I made up a bed for him inside a cardboard box lined with a soft blanket. I cut a rectangle door flap in one side of the box, enabling him to come and go as he pleased, as well as providing a private spot he could retreat to. After a play session that night, Chief had a quick snack and headed for his hideout. That was the last I saw or heard from him until the morning.

Chief woke me for an early breakfast; a sample of organic chicken and gravy from the pet store. A cloud of starlings caught his eye and he ran to the large window in my living room to investigate. The starlings were unknowingly putting on a show for Chief. Laying down and settling into a warm spot in the sunlight, he conducted the starlings for the rest of the morning.

Recognizable Friends

October, November, December

Identifying Features

By mid October I had several crow visitors. It is now easier for me to identify a male or a female crow just by their initial behaviour. I was looking for distinguishing marks and was interested in how many regular crows were actually visiting the perch.

If you catch the moment of a crow in the right light and angle, you will see purple, blue, and even green shades in their plumage, not just jet black. Not all crows had identifying markings so I began to watch closely for anything I could find.

Spirit

Spirit was easily identifiable with his feather sticking up and I could recognize him just about anywhere except in flight. Spirit was first, always. Landing, strutting and flicking his whole coat, *"I am the boss here and don't forget it"*. He was amazing and never moved far away when I put food out.

He liked to circle back to take what I had just put out for another crow before it can even get out of its tree, just like his predecessor. He was just as trusting towards me too and rarely moved off the perch as I came near. As I stood back and still, he'd come bouncing up and didn't mind me being that close to him when he picked up his treats.

Jack & Mr. & Mrs. Crow

I was still on the lookout for Jack, or any other crow who could perform the corner jump like he did. I keep wondering about Mr. Crow and Mrs. Crow too, but they still were no where to be seen, I hoped they are doing okay.

Hoppy

An unexpected visitor appeared on the garage roof, in exactly the same place I had fed the injured seagull, was this Hoppy? I think so as he didn't even flinch when I approached the railing, whereas a seagull on the garage roof would fly off immediately as soon as I opened the kitchen door.

Standing tall and confident, a lovely full grown seagull. Full white plumage, perfect grey wings, dappled tail and one leg slightly shorter than the other.

It must be him, he knew (or he remembered?) the food routine well. He waited patiently for me to throw something to him on the roof. It was nice to see him again, it kind of made up for the crow loss.

Elders

I had not seen as much of the elders as I would have liked. Perhaps they could be keeping an eye on things from a nearby position and had not been noticed, purposely staying further back. They may only visit in the fall and winter I don't know. Hopefully they show up again soon.

Standing out on my balcony just before lunch time, I saw two Elders perched as a pair in the nearby Maple tree, looking directly at me. They are easy for me to spot now, very regal and slightly bigger than Spirit. Unassuming, gracious movements and just as trusting as when I had first met them. They have a way of sitting back leaning against the base of their tail feathers with their claws over the front of the railing, the others don't land or sit like that. I called it the *'Statue Position'*. Unless they were leaving, the only thing that moved were their eyes, other than the occasional slow single blink.

I wondered why they were here. Possibly a hospitality check up, seeing if personal service is still available for a winter full of crow activity once again. I said ***"You are welcome here anytime and all these crows are welcome. If I knew your name I'd call it but I don't ... Hello anyway"***, then I blinked both eyes slowly. Not having much to say to me, I came back inside to prepare a little something special for them. They eagerly took the raw strips of liver I placed across the brushed off perch. They loved that, I think they're convinced, and they can't take it all. Pausing a moment for another double blink, a nod to say thank you, and making sure they had the best grip on their treats. *"Drop in anytime"*, I said. They took off, maybe looking for a safe landing spot to eat and were soon out of sight.

These elders are not to be mistaken for Ravens, which are considerably larger with different overall characteristics.

Starlings & Chief

I added a few organic treats to the regular Crow's diet and realized that I was probably feeding a dozen of them now. They all still went somewhere first thing in the morning, and showed up here anytime after 9:00 am. There were up to 300 to 400 starlings around daily, no matter the weather.

I could throw a double handful of cat kibble out on the balcony or the lawn and it would be gone in seconds. When a cloud of starlings changes directions in the air it creates a unique visual pattern. This fascinated Chief and it quickly became his new favourite pastime.

Hunter

I only noticed Hunter's tracks after a fresh snow, indicating he was still around here somewhere. Specifically I came out one morning after a light snow and Hunter's paw prints were visible leading up the stairs, across the balcony railing and onto the crow's perch. There are still a few snow flakes in the air, these tracks are fresh, I haven't missed his presence by much. Maybe next time.

Other Birds

During the later months the other Seagulls only came around when I threw bread up onto my roof, so it really was mostly crows. A nearby family of Bluejays didn't seem interested in my balcony and I hardly saw any others except when they squawked through the area occasionally.

There were also a pair of Downy wood peckers that would drop in once in a while for a few crumbs.

Behaviours & Antics

This fall was much the same as the last, but with the antics of Spirit prevailing throughout. Spirit had a way of stepping back a couple of steps then would abruptly stop, and he'd look at me as if to say ***"Oh c'mon, you don't really expect me to believe that do you?"***. Flicking all his feathers ***"Where's the meat?"***. It's going to be an interesting winter with him around. Seagulls be forewarned.

Gifts

I did find an occasional beer bottle cap or an aluminum pop can tab. Sometimes a shiny piece of silver paper. Bringing what appeared to be tokens of their appreciation of the hospitality they were experiencing. These were often left on the perch or directly in their water dish early in the morning. I hadn't had the opportunity of actually seeing who brought these gifts to me.

Whenever I found a piece of metal or anything resembling a gift, I always made sure to put a slice of raw meat in its place to reciprocate the gesture.

Echo Check

November

On a misty November morning Spirit landed on the damp stairwell corner of the railing. I saw the flight path he used often to approach the garden with, I was sure it was him. ***"CAW CAW CAW"*** - It was so loud and penetrating that I thought he was in my kitchen for a moment.

I watched through the side of the door window curtain, unseen but seeing. Spirit barked out his call and then looked all around upwardly and expectantly …Twisting, turning and cocking his head in all different directions … He repeated the three caws again, which somehow were louder than the first. This time however his attention towards the sky was rewarded.

The sound of three clear loud caws could be heard in response from the distance. It came from the right of my house, over and beyond the neighbours rooftop. Spirit appeared to be very satisfied, turning around and hopping along the railing to where I would normally see him at.

"Honk Honk" - *"Anybody home?"* This time I was already there. The friend he signalled did not join Spirit. They appeared content to know each other were close by. I wondered who he was calling?

From his perspective I believe he thought *"Nobody knows I'm here yet, I'll just check in with a friend to let him know I'm over here in my garden"*.

Seeing His Shadow

December to January

The sunshine today was a welcome sight after the cold temperatures. It warmed up to minus 8 Celsius this afternoon. The weather forecast was predicting less snow this year than the previous Nor'easter storms. This meant there would be less snow on the ground overall for the time period of February and March. Last January began tamely as well. There was a mention of our first Nor'easter but that is a few days away yet.

A few of the crows that were here in the fall have departed. Spirit never left though. One morning hearing his food honk, I looked out of the window and saw him and what must have been his mate. There they were, together on the perch.

Before opening the screen door, Spirit flew into a nearby tree and she followed immediately, landing next to him. They both watched as I laid out a few strips of chicken skin on the perch; Spirit could not resist, leaping off the branch and landing on the perch. I slowly backed up inside the door frame and shut the screen door. At first I thought Spirit did not want the chicken skins, but actually he waited for her to land on the perch before beginning to eat. I must have missed the courtship because there is clearly a connection between these two.

I can see they are a couple, and Spirit appears quite proud of her. She looked immaculate, essentially flawless. I may be able to identify her later by her movements, as I see which branches she lands on as well as how she lands.

Crow activity and antics were very similar to last year. The males coming right onto the perch, ready to dive in and the females waiting for the click of the door being closed. Spirit would come right up to my window, looking inside, and honk until I came out. He is amazing. Again I would like to emphasize their evident gestures of appreciation, Spirit says thank you almost like a gentleman tipping his hat.

As I opened the door she flew up onto a tree branch without a sound. I said *"Congratulations Spirit she looks like a perfect match"*. I came back inside and as soon as the door clicked closed she came down to the perch to join her new friend. If he landed on the perch or flew onto a certain branch, so did she, following him everywhere, shadowing his every move. After a few days of seeing this I started calling her Shadow. They made a lovely pair.

Elders Council

January

On the third Saturday in January close to lunch time, it began to snow heavily as I returned home from the farmers market. After parking my car I loaded myself up with groceries and made my way to the top of the stairs.

With a few steps left to go, I noticed a unique looking crow I recognized as being an Elder type. Just hanging out, calmly perched on the corner pillar. Sitting in about an inch of snow. This was the highest point of the balcony. I don't think he'd been there very long.

I was quite surprised to see him there. I slowed right down as I approached him. I said ***"Hey there, ..Hello, Hello.. Welcome to the balcony. Are we getting a storm?"***. He didn't move as I walked passed him, being only a few inches away from me. He didn't even stand up, just sitting there all puffed out.

He did acknowledge my greeting with a few slow blinks. No sound though, keeping a watchful eye on me. Had he come to warn me about the first Nor'easter of the season?

I came back out and cleared the railing slowly. I put a piece of kidney where I would normally have put it, about three feet away from him, he could clearly see it. As I stepped up backwards into my kitchen this crow just walked up slowly and casually, adjusted his grip on the slice of kidney with his beak then looked up and said thank you before taking off with it. I wondered when I might see him or her again.

Feather Box

January

A while back I had started collecting feathers by picking up any black feather that was near perfect. Eventually I had a full collection of wing feathers, tail feathers and lots of various smaller ones. I initially put them in a big brown envelope but I wanted a way to provide better protection for them. I had picked up a rectangular wooden box that had a clasp on it from a yard sale at the end of last summer. I thought it would fit the feather shape well, so when I got it home, I carefully transferred my collection into it.

It had been overcast all morning, and started out at minus 8 Celsius with a heavy snow warning for later. After a coffee and a piece of toast with marmalade, I put my parka on intending to go out for a quick walk before the storm struck. I went down my stairs and around the back garden under the trees. I was hoping to find a discarded feather or two if I was lucky enough, or some fresh Hunter tracks under the branches where the crows perched so often. You never know when and where a feather may turn up.

While there were no stray cat tracks to be found, on my way inside just below the corner of the garage roof overhang, I found a prize wing feather. I came inside and brought it over to Chief. His eyes lit up and dove head first for a sniff. I gave him a minute to get the crows scent. Placing a paw on the feather, he looked at me for a moment without a meow. He carefully watched as I put the feather away in the box, then lowered it to let him sniff all the feathers at once. His eyes glazed over and he entered what seemed to be a deep feather trance. I closed the lid but this didn't break the spell. He followed me as I entered my living room.

After taking a phone call I returned to the living room and noticed I had unintentionally left the feather box out on the coffee table. Well it could have been worse. Thankfully he hadn't gotten the lid off. Chief was lying beside it, stretched out with one paw draped over one corner and the other one around the back of it. He was gently and slowly rubbing his whiskers against the corner of the box, purring heavily. His eyes were glazed over and both front paws were kneading imaginary dough.

Chief was still in some kind of trance. His eyes didn't respond to me passing my hand in front of them. I called him a few times, *"Chief, Chief, ..Chief"*, finally an eyelid flickered. I called him again *"Chief?"*. He seemed to awaken from the feather trance, letting out a few marbled meows. The smell of all those feathers combined totally wiped him out and he was in la-la land there for sure.

Chief looked at me and said *"Marrrowww"* very sleepily; I took it to mean *"I love those feathers"*. As I picked the box up he wanted to go with it, so I gave him a nice full feather of his own to distract him. He rolled all over it continuously.

The weather began to pick up as ice pellets started to fall just before lunch. Through the kitchen window I can see the wind blowing the hail and sleet almost sideways, but I do not see any crows, I wonder where they are taking shelter? Five hours later the temperature had gone up to 4 Celsius, changing the ice over to snow. It quickly ramped up to a heavy snow, then after an hour it softened back to a lighter snow again.

That evening I put Chief's feather next to his pillow, as it might help him sleep. It was still storming as I turned the lights out before retiring for the night. Chief is nestled quietly in his bed box right where I placed the feather. Good night.

Chapter Four

Magic In The Heir

The mystery and wonder
Turned into a friend,
A stranger at first
A king in the end.

Feather In The Weather

From February to July 2016

Everyone was looking forward to a friendlier winter this year. Thankfully the Winter Almanac had forecast a mild season compared to last year, with less frequent Nor'easters.

This gives me hope for a better environment for the crows to build a nest. A tree sheltered from the weather would be one consideration, another could be based on their decision to build near a supplementary food source.

It snowed from day one of 2016, unlike last year with nothing until the end of the month. We've already had one surprise this January and several particularly cold days. February I'm sure has its itinerary in store with things kicking off with a few snowflakes tomorrow morning.

The crows had clearly demonstrated their cycle of adaptability thus far. They seemed impervious to any weather conditions. They are as active in the winter as they are in warmer months. Being out in wind, rain and snow didn't seem to phase them. It's all about food.

Beast From Nor'East

February

A Nor'easter is set to hit Nova Scotia this Monday, and the weather report has forecast as much as 50 centimetres of snow with heavy blizzard conditions. They are calling for very high wind speeds. This could be a bad one. Just popping outside to look around and a sudden gust of wind just about took my screen door off. Looking in the distance, I can see the dark clouds approaching from the horizon from over the lakes.

I would describe a Nor'easter as a hurricane but with snow, sleet, and hail instead of rain. They often affect Nova Scotia and other Atlantic provinces and some eastern coast states in the winter months. Winds associated with these storms can cause the snow to drift, which can double the accumulated snow where ever the drift meets an object.

The snow flakes have begun. They are small which usually means a lot of snow. An old saying goes something like this *"Big flake = little snow; little flake = big snow"*. The winds have picked up now, with strong gusts causing the siding and roof to whistle as it wraps around the corners of the house. I am cooking a roast beast and mashed potatoes with gravy for dinner and hunkering in for the night.

During a Nor'easter, it's every creature for itself. There are usually no birds willing to risk trying to fly and navigate in such a storm. The wind was easily strong enough for a crow to glide itself in on the wind, appearing almost stationary to Chief and I as we looked through the window, watching it hover. Chief was absolutely fascinated by this, he wanted to be a part of it all.

I knew from last season that a crow was capable of doing a glide-in landing with only a few steps to balance. The wind is highly capable of blasting the same crow right off the perch after landing, which is why I started throwing food onto the garage roof for them in extraordinarily strong weather.

During one of the Nor'easter storms, while looking out of the kitchen window, I noticed Mr. Crow flying directly into the wind and snow, in an attempt to land on my balcony railing. I could see him hovering a few seconds before making a smooth landing.

It seemed like a work of art to be able to land on a wooden railing with nothing for their feet to clutch around in a strong gusty wind. The experience and skill it must have taken to pull that off reminded me of seeing a jet landing on an aircraft carrier using resting cables and tail hooks in storm force winds.

I wouldn't usually put anything on the perch in a storm unless there was an incredibly brave crow lurking about. Right on cue, Spirit was determined to lead by example, I can see Spirit and Shadow clinging to a lower tree branch near the trunk of a Maple tree, trying to keep their balance. I took out the trimmings collected from the roast I prepared earlier, and paused before opening my screen door.

The wind was picking up, I knew I had to be quick and careful or I would lose the door to the wind. Trying to open my screen door against the wind is almost impossible. Opening the door into the wind could result in it overstraining the hinges and being slammed against the railing.

I held the door as firmly as I could with my left hand. As soon as I cracked it open just enough to get my right foot outside on the balcony, the wind caught it, ripping it from my hand, causing it to crash into the railing. The door stayed pressed against the railing as I put some food onto the perch against the water dish to give it some support in the wind. I came inside and closed my door as Spirit showed up but the wind was too strong for him to land so he did a snatch-by.

Chief couldn't get any closer or he would have been outside. Watching from the kitchen window sill he saw Spirit approaching from the right. Spirit was gliding in as he adjusted his equipment to just the right angles and settings. While being blasted by driving snowflakes, he managed to fly alongside and slightly above the perch. Hovering there for a few seconds, then without touching the perch, he tipped himself down enough to grab whatever he could in his beak. With Chief looking on, he soared up into the oncoming wind and went with it instead of against it. It was well timed for the circumstances. Chief had his front paws on the window pane being pummelled by sleet and snow. *"C'mon Chief, let's make some hot chocolate, it's going to be a nasty night for some"* I said. Chief was happy to get his roast dinner plate and stayed in his bed box for most the night.

Chief made sure I was up early this morning. After we had our breakfast, I joined him by the living room window. Today started as a complete white out, everything is covered by more than a foot of snow. It is a winter wonderland as far as the eye can see. There is a rough shape of my car under the drift, and all the roof tops, tree branches and power lines are coated in a glaze of ice.

The snow piled so high from the wind drifts that Chief could not see out of the kitchen window. The screen door will not open more than an inch, I guess that means I'm staying in for the day? As the sun peaked at noon, it softened the snow blocking my door enough for me to dig my way out to stand on the balcony. It took an hour to clear off the top of the balcony, railings, and the perch. With temperatures going to minus 5 overnight, I am glad I picked up an extra bag of road salt as the deck will get slippery as it freezes tonight.

Watch Tower

March

The crows loved peanuts in the shell. I often toss a couple in the direction of any crows I see as I descend my staircase to the driveway. Sometimes out of my car window as I am leaving. I also do the same thing when I come back up the road to my driveway.

Crows are incredibly smart and it wasn't long before they began to identify my car. They also eventually realized that those white plastic bags I am often bringing from it, probably contained something for them.

"He's leaving the house and getting in his car" soon meant, **"He's probably going grocery hunting and bringing stuff back for us too"**.

It was after lunch and had been raining quite steadily. I was coming back up the hill to where I lived but made a brief stop at the mailboxes about halfway up. Before I got there I could see a crow sentinel perched on a power pole close by near the mailbox corner. He looked drenched but was still on duty. I stopped the car, got out with my mail key and looked up at the crow on top of the pole.

I thought that he was probably on watch duty, his job was to notice things and pass the message on by calling out loudly so the next crow would hear it. *"Caww Caww, Caww Caww"* he relayed. Well I didn't realize at that point that I was the message.

After retrieving my mail and getting back in the car, my sentinel swooped ahead quite low and deliberately as I pulled away from the curb. As I approached my turn into the driveway he turned up and right at the same time, circling back behind me. He landed on the wires stretching across from the top of the house and the garden pole. Two others flew into a nearby Maple tree to join him. I could see that my two main crows - Spirit and Shadow, were already on the perch as I got out of the car. I was impressed, it seemed very well orchestrated.

While carrying several bags of groceries, I turned the corner at the top of my stairs and Shadow took off to a nearby favourite branch. I opened the screen door and accidentally banged the bags down as I was getting the door key out, causing Spirit to take off as well. I propped the screen door open so I could use both hands to carry the bags inside. With the doors still open I stepped out onto the balcony to take a quick look around. Spirit landed near the far corner and was looking at me as if to say *"Do you think there is enough for all of us?"*.

I looked around at this welcoming committee with visibly expectant crows lined up in different spots. There were seven of them in all. This couldn't have transpired by mere individual action, this was a joint effort and the crows seemed quite excited that it had gone according to their plan.

Crows have a way of letting you know that they are pleased and make clicking noises. They exude different body postures and flick their feathers and shake themselves. It's very amusing to watch.

And yes I did have one of their favourites, fresh beef liver, which was greatly appreciated by all concerned. It was all gone within a couple of minutes.

It's highly likely that there are crows on watch in certain strategic places, just observing things. Keeping watch for us, always ready to cleanup any roadkill or attending to some other very important business.

I must say it was a pleasant surprise to have my own personal crow entourage escorting me into my driveway. It was a very welcoming greeting. By now, they know me and they know my car. My next door neighbour came over to comment on what she had seen. She had been watching from her driveway and saw all these crows arriving together, taking up close positions right before I showed up.

Crows Be Cawtious

Late March, April

Aside from an assortment of toys he got in his stocking, Chief's main gift this year was a new red halter and a matching leash that I picked up online. As the last of the snow melted away, I thought it was the right time to put the halter on Chief as he seemed very interested in going outside to check things out. With a brief sniff-check and a roll of approval to let me know he liked it, he was ready to put it on. I took him out with his halter connected to the leash, we went down the stairs, paused there for a few minutes while he sniffed about as we enjoyed the smell of the fresh spring air.

I encouraged him to walk with me onto the front lawn, but as soon we got there it began to rain. Chief instinctively bolted for the stairs. I didn't want to hold him back so I let go of the leash; at top speed he ran back up the stairs to my balcony. I had propped the screen door open so he let himself inside. The expression on his face was half wonder and half relief to be back inside. After getting the halter off I gave him a few treats to reward his bravery.

I noted that the crows only sounded the alarm if any of the next door cats were actually in my garden, under or close to the perch. Otherwise they were quiet.

The crows didn't seem to know what to make of this creature with different colors, nevertheless they knew it was some kind of cat and remained cautious until he was inside.

I continued to take my cat out for familiarization walks around the back of the house and garden, around the garage, as well as the front of the house. I wanted him to be very familiar with his surroundings before the summer so I would be able to let him roam freely in the garden.

After about two weeks I started to let Chief off the leash for a while as I walked beside him but as soon as he looked lost or a bit confused I'd put it back on. One day I decided to allow him to roam the garden, I unclipped his leash and let him go, to my surprise he came back fairly soon all by himself. Becoming more comfortable with his surroundings, he seemed thoroughly excited that it was his garden too. Not unlike a brand new kitten or puppy getting their first romp in the yard, Chief still had a kitten like wonder about the outdoors.

After all this time inside he was not a hunting cat anymore and just wanted to be outside with the rest of the animals. The crows knew he was with the good guy, but he was still a cat. I really hadn't given much thought to the five cats or the drifter cat as I hadn't expected that my cat would want to go outside. I knew it was possible but I thought it unlikely that they would all be outside together.

As soon as my cat saw one of the five, he just sat down wherever he was and kept still. Eventually this secret tactic produced phenomenal results. Not one fight, not even a squabble with any of them and in a couple more weeks, they all knew each other and had become friends.

On a Monday just before lunch, I was wondering where my cat was and looked outside. He was sitting at the top of my stairs looking down at the stray cat. Has Chief charmed Hunter using the same secret tactic? As soon as I appeared Chief stood his ground as Hunter bolted for the back of the garage somewhere. Nevertheless they had met. I didn't see much of him at all. Hunter wasn't a problem to us.

Evergreen Castle

April

I admit that the thought of another possible nest building had crossed my mind more than once. In mid April I noticed that there were four crows that were busy on the ground under the trees sorting and gathering suitable nest building materials.

I observed some of it was going to the left somewhere and some going to the right. Anything going to my left was hard to keep track of and I couldn't tell where it was actually going. They were picking up and dropping twigs and sticks, the same as the previous year. I was expecting and hoping that a nest may be built somewhere as close as the first one from the previous year.

There are a pair of crows building a nest in the trees growing on the property to my left, I wonder who they are? I guess the neighbours five cats did not deter them from choosing this nesting site. I know where the nest is roughly but from my balcony, as I look in that direction it's out of my viewing area; while Spirit and Shadow, as I called them, are building somewhere to my right.

I really got quite curious and kept a close watch on the situation. I finally saw Shadow, after picking up a suitable twig, take off and fly directly up to my right to the group of older but very tall white pine trees in the far corner of the property. The nest is wedged between the trunk and a double forked horizontal branch. Being at a lower elevation than the tops of the other trees in the cluster this offered the nest far better protection from the elements. It seemed to be well hidden from above too.

So they're building there, just beyond the garage. I decided to stand outside to get a wider view than just looking into my garden from the window. The position of the nest is high up but still better protected than the solitary maple tree used by Mr. and Mrs. Crow. The foundation for the nest was well on its way.

I did notice the exception of any additional helpers this time, or maybe they were out of my line of sight blocked by the garage. Seeing the grass going in meant it must be almost finished, and soon enough Shadow was sitting and Spirit was on guard.

I was so pleased to know where they were, and taking into account the recent cat activity around my house, it was a safer choice for all in question. The conditions were better than last year, at least there were real buds on the trees and they seemed committed this time. Shadow sat and Spirit guarded. I came out first thing one morning to look at the nest and there was no one on it, then I saw Shadow cruise in and take up position again.

There was still some inclement weather, but crows are tough and tenacious. Even after all the wind and rain, she never gave up. Both showing up here daily at the perch, sodden and soaked through, but they stuck it out and stayed with the nest. I was hopeful.

My rough calculation was that there would be hatchings soon if there were going to be any at all. It was more than 21 days now. I didn't know how many days were taken to lay the eggs or how many eggs there were.

Garden Guards

Overall it had been a busy winter. There must have been up to about 15 crows in all. I had about eight to ten regular crow visitors with the rest dropping in for a winter snack now and again.

There were numerous seagull skirmishes. If a high flying seagull scout notices any kind of accentuated crow activity, it's coming in to investigate and will have soon summoned additional help.

These occurrences are more common than I expected, and are usually comprised of a marauding band of always hungry seagulls trying their luck on the railing or the garage roof, it didn't matter where. Depending upon the bounty in question a group of seagulls will crash land right in the middle of anything, followed by its accompaniment and will steal and devour anything that will fit into their mouths, and, they vanish in seconds. They would eat crow eggs if they could find some.

Understandably, the crows are not putting up with any more of that than they have to and are quick to activate their own *'Personal Food Supply'* defence system which consists of calling in every immediate crow available ready to fight. As far as who can summon the most troops at one time as quickly as they do I have to give the edge to the crows.

The majority of the time, it was the same dominant male Spirit and his immediate colleagues on the scene, they ran the show. It appeared that it was *'Their Garden'*.

Cat's Curiosity

May

Chief was getting very curious now. I'd find him sitting on the kitchen window ledge face pressed against the glass, watching the crows land on the perch. ***"No, no, he's our friend"*** I'd say, lifting him backwards a few inches. Well you can only explain so much to a cat. Chief had some other ideas and plans of his own.

The crows had learned that they always needed to be facing my stairs when landing on the perch, just to keep an eye or two on things. Chief came leaping up them one morning, right up to the perch with a crow on it. Fortunately it was Spirit, whom, I thought was understanding in these matters. Chief must have seen him from the driveway and could this be the opportunity he was dreaming of?

Spirit was already three feet away backwards before Chief had reached the top stair, but didn't mind moving just in case. I brought him inside, *"You rascal"* I told him, *"Let me guess, you just wanted another feather for your collection?"*.

The very next day I heard the alarm again coming from outside on the balcony. It was Spirit cawing at my cat, perched about two feet above him this time on the railing. Chief was so close he couldn't stand it anymore and sunk into a spring position ready to pounce. Spirit easily lifted himself backwards and upwards out of harms way, onto an awaiting branch. *"KWAAARK!"*

This was not a frantic warning or a general alarm call. It was more of an *"WHAT? HA! You'll have to do much better than that"*.

The sound of it was loud and coarse like a single elongated cat warning burst with just one utterance. One long loud CAW, these crows have volume when they need it.

Knowing that I was trying to keep the cat away from them, as soon as I had the cat safely inside, down he came now that the coast was clear.

By the time all the snow had melted, I think the crows and my cat had come to some kind of an arrangement. They had gotten to know each other, thankfully to a peaceful result. They all seemed to have developed a mutual respect for each other. Chief was really trying to understand everything.

The crows seem to still be on alert, to avoid any potential danger like the stray cat or a roaming osprey.

Historical Hatching

June

The buds were bursting out into a now ever growing landscape of emerald greens and fresh spring colors. In a couple of weeks time the foliage would obscure my view of the nest completely.

I was watching the nest early one morning through my binoculars. Swiftly Shadow landed with a mouthful, and four baby beaks popped up above the nest line. Their mouths sprung wide open. ***"Me first!" - "No me, no me, I was first!"***

A percussion of chirps was silenced as each got their share. I was thrilled there was new life. Spirit and Shadow are parents now.

I had been keeping a close watch on exactly who was coming to the perch. I counted seven in all. There was Spirit and Shadow, and another arrogant young male with his mate, who had a white band in almost the same place as the grey one on Shadow. I expect the other two were the previous nesters from last year, could it really be Mr. & Mrs. Crow returning? Perhaps they had been successful this time around in a different location. The male was very comfortable with me being there close to him and stayed on the railing when I put some food out and she'd land as soon as I closed the door.

The other three adult crows were coming to the perch as well with the seventh very likely being a younger male compared to the rest. He wasn't first, but did jump in front of the females when the other males flew away.

Spirit was getting crafty as I'd only give him so much, he'd land on a different branch to make me think he was a different crow. Maybe something to do with a new family to support.

Feeding on the perch was intensifying, two new busy mothers by the looks of it, one I knew of for sure. Shadow landed with the door closed. I watched as she took a bite and seemed to have swallowed it but then followed by a small drink of water, and again more food and then more water, this was repeated until her throat looked very full. She was mixing water with the food presumably to make it easier to regurgitate the food for the chicks. The other female is doing exactly the same thing. Spirit doesn't do this, which leads me to believe he's not taking part in the feeding.

I can't wait to see the little ones. These guys are growing fast and are filling the whole nest. There are no domestic cats near the nest, just the possibility of the stray cat passing by on one of his excursions. I am unable to see the nest at all now, it's completely obscured by leaves from the overlapping Maple branches. The chicks looked really big the last time I saw them. I'm sure there isn't enough room for all of them in there at the same time. I hope no one gets pushed out. I'll just have to wait now and see who shows up. It won't be long before they are out of the nest if they aren't already.

The thought of having Mr. and Mrs. Crow back with us again was encouraging as well as them possibly celebrating their own season's success story. It is clear both Mrs. Crow and Shadow are loading up with food and water before departing from the perch.

A few days had gone by now. After lunch one day, I noticed a strange crow had landed to the far right of the garage roof. It was strange because I hadn't seen any crows land there before. It was also facing away from the deck. I was about to throw it a treat, only to see Spirit swoop down and chase it away. It must have been an intruder from somewhere. I had not seen him chase any crows away before.

Defence From Above

June

The nest building hasn't gone unnoticed. Spirit has been busy chasing away any perceived threats from above. One morning before lunch, I watched from my balcony through binoculars as a seagull had flown too close for comfort, according to Spirit. Before leaving his position in the nesting tree, Spirit cawed once **"CAAWWW"**, then launched himself toward the invader at full speed.

The wandering seagull was circling slowly around the area, dropping altitude when it became aware of the squawking crow approaching quickly. The seagull was completely surprised; I saw it veer off and away as two helpers appeared and joined in after it from behind, screeching loudly as they went.

It smoothly zig-zagged above the rooftops until it had disappeared out of my sight. The crows followed it beyond my vision, but only Spirit returned a few minutes later quietly back onto my garage roof where I rewarded him with a few treats.

Spirit was not afraid to get involved with an Osprey or two. I had observed that there are two pairs of Osprey that live in the woods beyond the lake of which is due east from here. I've often heard them calling while circling high above slowly moving out over the bigger lakes. They occasionally cross over this area but appear to purposely avoid my garden, possibly because Mr. Crow had chased one away last year.

Anything in close proximity to the nest was enough for Spirit to immediately investigate. Calling for backup as he did. Spirit would often climb higher than the invader and dived directly at it making a lot of fuss and noise as he did. He would confront his enemy physically and verbally. The intruder would either be knocked or bothered off course until it was sufficiently deterred. Visibly its course will be altered steering it away from the the danger zone. Spirit always waited to ensure the invading alien had left the area or for his back up to arrive and be welcomed.

I was always awe struck when a bunch of supporting crows would materialize seemingly from nowhere to help out. In the calls that followed I imagined that Spirit thanked his cohorts for their effort. They would circle around the area for several minutes making their vocal presence known until the sky's were safe again. I probably missed the sound for the *"All clear"*.

Most of the threats to their eggs or young came from above. As for below, the only perceived danger around here would be Hunter, the stray cat.

Training Days

June to July

Learning To Fly

Late this morning I heard a weak sounding, solitary caw, one at a time, coming from close by. Upon investigation it was a baby crow sitting in a tree in my garden just to the left of the garage roof. It sounded unsure, learning to talk, no power yet unlike its highly vocal parents.

The baby crow was in fact two babies talking to each other. Up until then, I had not seen the second one, which was sitting a little higher than the first. They just sat there, getting up every now and then to stretch their legs and wings.

Their training may not have been scheduled that morning but they were practicing what they had learned while getting used to their balancing act. They were hopping from branch to branch with wings out, eagerly but still unable to fly properly yet. The feathers in their wings and tails were not fully developed either which was preventing them from taking full advantage of the wind.

Shadow would go from the perch onto the branch the babies were on and pop some food into an expectant mouth. She would then take off to somewhere else, presumably feeding the other babies wherever they were; or reloading for more.

I think the mothers will continue feeding the young up to and during their first winter.

The babies are jump-flying from branch to branch and seem limited as to the actual distance they can fly. They just need some time to acquaint and familiarize themselves with their environment as well as their developing equipment.

First thing this morning 6:15 am, a baby crow landed in a tree over the garage roof. Shadow followed it here so I threw a drumstick onto the roof. She took the drumstick and flew off towards the lake. I threw another drumstick and the baby landed onto the roof. The fledgling is not sure about the drumstick but takes it anyway and flies off in Shadow's direction.

After a period of about five minutes, a fledgling I hadn't noticed earlier, jumped down to a lower branch in the tree closest to the garage. I threw a slice of beef onto the garage roof fairly close to the youngster, it did nothing, it just sat there looking around.

A larger second crow sailed in and landed about a foot away from the first. The second crow turned out to be the Mum, it was Shadow and a baby. The baby started to sidle up to her, but she called something out *"Caaw!"* and the youngster did a 180 degree turn on the branch. Shadow then proceeded to bump the chick right off the branch onto the garage roof!

It flapped and flopped as it landed, proceeding to take the food I had thrown to it earlier. Shadow then took off and the rattled baby followed. So this is how they learn, I was amazed. Shadow is training right in front of me. Todays curriculum/lesson plan appears to be: If there is food nearby then it is better to go get it, not just look at it!

Vocals 101

It was a quiet and sunny morning early in July. I see the roses and orchids around the garden have opened up for the sun. The roses bearing a deep ruby red and the orchids showing off a vibrant white and purple in direct sunlight.

I had my kitchen door open as it was already warming up outside. As soon as I heard the first sounds my attention was engaged. These were different sounds, I had to check it out and see for myself.

The sounds were from a crow outside cawing quite softly, these were the softest close range calls I have ever heard. Overlapping it are two more different-toned 3-caw-calls.

Looking outside I traced the calls to Shadow and two youngsters in a maple tree close to the back fence. It appears they are in class getting verbal instruction from their mother.

She is making a call and the two students were doing their best to mimic her by repeating it. There are only two youngsters here out of four, I wonder where the other two are.

Shadow is calling softly, giving them a basic three caw call - *"caw..caw..caw"*;

"Caw Caw Caw", a little more volume on that one;

"CAW CAW CAW!" even louder, then back down to soft again *"caw caw caw"*.

This is amazing. Crow school right in front of me. Mum is teaching advanced volume control and what the different levels of power mean in crow speak. The youngsters are trying that level of volume or power when reciting it back to her.

Practicing together, this lasted for several minutes. I hope I get to see more of this. Practice makes perfect. All the volume from these young ones added up wouldn't compete with a single power blast from Mr. Crow or Spirit, the adults can be very loud when they want to be.

Follow The Leader

It occurred to me that at this time my cat was sitting about four steps down on my staircase, yet no alarms were given. Today, just a few moments ago, four crows landed in the same tree. They arrived together. Having tufty feathers sticking out all over the place, they were clearly youngsters. I threw some food onto the garage roof. One flew down and took the food then flew off towards a patch of trees in the distance. Chief was quietly taking it all in, without making a sound or movement.

I threw another piece of food on the garage roof. This enticed a second youngster to land with the third one following behind it. Immediately opening its mouth to be fed, squawking loudly. The second youngster took off with the food. Before I could throw anymore food onto the roof, the other two flew off as well. This all happened fifteen feet away from me with my kitchen door wide open.

Partially because of my cat but mostly not wanting to create a dependency, I had no intention of feeding baby crows on the perch or to entice them to it. Yet, that is what happened anyway. These youngsters are inexperienced and unaware of the potential dangers related to cats. Anything that would go onto the garage roof was totally impossible for any kitty to get at.

I spotted a fledgling exploring the garage roof, hopping across the shingles. As I came to the door it took off into a close by tree. After putting a treat out on the perch for Spirit, I came back in and closed the door. Seconds later, Spirit landed briefly on the corner of the perch. He quickly grabbed the treat and departed.

I guess that it's monkey see monkey do for some behaviours, because a young crow just landed on the perch with nothing on it except a water dish. He wasn't waiting. I had no chance to put anything else out yet since Spirit took the last. As I came outside the youngster flew off into a tree and I put a piece of treat on the perch that was clearly visible. In closing the door I saw him land on the railing and approached the perch hesitantly. I knew he could see it. Still unsure yet decisively taking the meat, he flew off and away towards the direction of where Spirit went.

About thirty minutes later he came back onto the railing and carefully approached the perch again, nervously looking for more treats. I would estimate this youngster as being a male as it is already exhibiting a daring persona from the get go. My cat was safely inside, just observing, occasionally chattering at the window.

New Found Fledglings

It would appear that there were four baby crows from the Evergreen Castle to my right and three more from the unseen nest of Mr. & Mrs. Crow to my left. It was only a matter of time before these all got together which is when I noticed a few differences between them. The first four are very black, just the same as Spirit and

Shadow. Opposed to the other three that are a combination of being a very dark brown and black. An untrained eye would have a hard time distinguishing which parents they belong to.

The black fledglings looked like baby crows. The browner ones had an almost chicken face appearance and seem to have a more streamlined build. Even having food right in front of them, one of them is still begging and squawking to be fed with its mouth wide open. The inside of their mouth is noticeably pink but will turn totally black as they get a little older. This particular young crow is either a late bloomer or perhaps crows have 'runts'?

I had already cut the availability of food to a minimum as I expected that both Mums would be teaching the youngsters how and where to find food for themselves. They do eat a lot of naturally available food. I didn't want to encourage any kind of dependancy from my supply.

During the winter, being fed or not, it seemed to be a habit or necessity for crows to attack garbage bags curbside. I always covered the bag with an old duvet cover to keep the crows off it or they'd tear it apart and drag stuff out in search of food. I never did this in June as the crows didn't bother with garbage bags this time of year and there was no need to search for food.

I had just put my black garbage bag on the sidewalk by the main road and once back inside, I just happened to glance at it from my living room window.

I watched as Shadow and four fledglings landed on my front lawn. Shadow went straight for this garbage bag and began digging at it and pulling stuff out with the youngsters watching.

One youngster leapt straight in before the others had a chance, after a few moments they all joined in like it was a huge game or something. To look for food this way was totally unnecessary at this time of year. Shadow was teaching the garbage bag drill, I had to laugh at the situation even though they made quite a mess for me to clean up.

Spirit and Shadow are showing up again individually and as a pair. I see much less of Mr. & Mrs. Crow as a pair although they are still visiting often. The oncoming summer is overtaking their breeding season and things are going to be much quieter. It must be nice for them to receive their treats in peace and quiet, without contending with all the other crows.

This past few weeks has seen all these fledglings developing into young crows ready to take their places in crow society. How many and who will I meet this Fall?

Will there be a new allocation, is my garden up for grabs? Who decides? Further more, what's going to happen to the reign of Spirit and Shadow, where are they going, where are they all going? Remembering how quiet it was last summer. Have Spirit and Shadow passed some kind of a test and are getting a promotion? I wonder how it all works.

Prospecting

August

Yesterday, while I was sitting out on the deck catching some rays, a thought occurred to me that this may be a good time to try a little experiment.

It was mid summer and had become reasonably quiet as far as crows were concerned. Wherever they had all gone to for the summer remains a mystery.

Having run out of liver and any other fresh meat scraps, I was feeding the few crows that were around with some high quality freeze dried free-run chicken that Chief would not eat. It's been a few days since I gave them raw meat, so this would be a good time to test a theory I had. How long it would take for the first crow to communicate to any others that there were meat treats being offered again on the perch. Would this information be passed on or would it be kept a secret?

I wasn't expecting any crows to be landing on the perch because of the increased outside cat presence from next door. They were all familiar with the garage rooftop which was really just a great big perch to them.

On the following Saturday, at about 1:15 pm, I sliced some fresh liver I had picked up specifically for crow treats. I was waiting for a crow to show up. Aha, I didn't have to wait very long for the first crow to appear. I noticed that familiar black shape gliding silently, landing in one of the trees at the back of the garage. Presuming it was a female as it didn't turn around and face the house as a male usually does.

I threw a piece of liver onto the garage roof, not expecting her to come much closer with me out on my deck. I couldn't really miss the roof, so anywhere was relatively good. Down she came and walked up to the food, picked it up, then took off towards the lake. I wondered how many might come? Did the others notice my sudden arm movement, or had a sentry spotted something from afar?

It wasn't very long, maybe less than a full minute, when the second crow which I recognized as having been here before. He showed up and had no problem dropping off his branch collecting his reward and departing.

Within five minutes nine different crows had showed up. They seemed to arrive from all different directions and departed much the same way. I think it's a pot luck guess as to how they know there's food here. Do they fly in the direction of their closest relatives or friends to share with? I doubt very much but maybe a case of ***"Well you'd better get over there asap and get some"***? There's a strong possibility that they are simply very observant and also have a cumulative intelligence regarding anything edible. Or maybe they have a better sense of smell than we give them credit for. This certainly isn't anything like a normal seasonal feeding frenzy with the same crows performing or new mothers with concerted roles to play.

Crow's Canvas

August

I was getting better at identifying them by now. Their visual appearance, their antics and upon which branch, and even in which tree they landed.

In the past it had come to my attention that wherever the crows went early in the morning, it was hazardous to them. They'd be showing up with paint streaks on them, on their legs, or head or somewhere. I saw one with totally white feet one morning.

Just the other day Spirit showed up with yellow paint all over his head, I mean a lot. Later in the same day he showed up again soaking wet as though it had been raining, which it hadn't, with the paint washed away he was a new crow again.

Somehow he had gotten a shower or a bath and was all clean again. He seemed very happy with his accomplishment, and he was strutting his stuff. He was puffing himself out, walking up and down flicking his feathers. As if to say *"Look at me"*. It was amusing.

Most of the time this paint or whatever they'd been digging through wore off fairly quickly. Occasionally it just faded leaving almost a scar of grey which I've noticed can last much longer before eventually fading away completely.

Males typically had specific behaviours such as elaborate approaches to the perch, or would peer in my window, what was he looking for? Whereas a female would descend quietly and unassumingly near the back part of the garden and face away from the perch and railing.

Ace of Spades

I can already see a clear leader shaping up from the original seven. To be more precise, he is Spirit and Shadow's son, or one of them.

Yesterday there were five young crows on the perch at the same time. One with both feet on the edge of the water dish making a racket, the highest point of the perch, a supposed position of towering dominance. Another contested his position with a few nudges, it could not budge him off the dish, eventually giving up.

"SQUAAARRRKK!!" was the only thing I heard for an introduction as the sixth young crow showed up by crash landing on the perch. The would-be perch keeper was knocked clean off the dish and right off the perch. Scattering everyone in the vicinity, making it perfectly clear to his peers who's dish it was. Indeed in his mind, it was his now.

There was something about him immediately. He was following his father's example. Not reckless. Yet easily identified now, not by anything except his attitude. *"I'm first, second - and third!"*

He's like two crows in one. I told my friend on the phone he has been hiding food and digging all over the place. Shovelling the dirt with his beak. He said I should get him a spade, *"That's it"* I said, *"Just like his father"*. He said what? *"The Ace of Spades. I'm calling him Ace for short."*

Crows re-hide their food if they see another crow watching and may repeat this process several times. *"I'll be back!"*

I expect I am going to be dealing with this guy later on. He's exhibiting all the traits and behaviours of the heir to the throne of this garden.

The first time Ace landed on the perch although hesitant he was there for a purpose, *"Where's my treat?"*. No fear, expectant and eager. He wasn't there for a social visit nor was he waiting. Ace really was a big chip off the old block. A fraction on the larger side compared to his siblings. Adept at gracefully athletic aerial displays at a few months old. No battle-scar feathers sticking out.

A unique specimen if there was to be only one. A flawless coat like his mother Shadow as if poured from a perfect mold. Who does he get his aristocratic poise from? Mum gets my vote on that one.

Continuously exhibiting fearless daring and bravery, but more calculated, it's *'Me first'* in a different light. Spirits vast knowledge as an experienced, mature and knowledgeable crow must be in his DNA. Whilst unknowingly wearing his fathers reputation. Ace is his own crow.

Seven Of Crows

Late August

The four fledglings from the Evergreen Castle and the three from Mr. & Mrs. Crow around the corner have grown up together.

These seven are closer connected to each other than the additional crows that they hang out with due to them being from this garden. I saw ten at once with Ace at the helm on more than one occasion. I knew there were another three as a group, that's his ten. Where the others are from exactly is unknown to me.

I've counted as many as 17 of these youngsters together at one time, hanging out and playing together over across the main road in a paved parking area. Now they are all lined up, single file along one power line. What are they up to?

As for the additional seven, other than occasionally meeting up with Ace's group along that power line across from my living room window, I did not see them around my garden, leaving me with no real information on them.

They could be seen in smaller groups together but the seven youngsters from my garden area were now seven as one.

This seemed to be a manageable number for them. The seven would raid my perch when it was supposedly quiet. It was a big game to them to see who could knock the water dish off the perch just for the fun of it. These crows had the audacity and were waiting for me to put the dish back after I had gone down the stairs and back.

Ace was usually at the forefront of these activities, or to put it in crow terms *'another one bites the dust'*. For the most part Ace was the leader, or instigator either in mischief or with good intentions. Enjoying his youth.

Looking For Mischief

Taking place on a warm, sunny and almost cloudless day, from my living room window I watched as Ace and his spades landed on the front lawn of my neighbours house with the five cats, looking for trouble.

I could see a bright ginger cat asleep on their front door step. Although being 20 percent of the total cat population, it was still only one cat.

The crows hadn't made a sound yet, they looked on as Ace edged even closer while ducking and hopping sideways. Only a few feet away, Ace was caught sneaking in as the supposed sleeping cat's head popped up unexpectedly.

Reacting automatically, Ace sprang sideways into a crouching crow fu stance. Seemingly uninterested, the sleepy cat watched Ace as he proceeded to hop in and out of range, and after a few moments laid his head back down.

Ace did a 180 direction change a few times before making his getaway. The other spectators all took off squarking together as they left, probably taunting the flightless cat. They're having fun together.

Water Park

A wet Saturday afternoon provided the ideal conditions for a bit of fun. The rain had stopped without warning, the sun now shone brightly yet everything was still dripping wet. I stepped outside to look around, and while standing at the corner of my balcony, I saw Ace as he led the detachment. Circling the garden at first, then flying past the house and across the street.

Splash landing into a puddle and flicking his wings, Ace proceeded to sit right down in the water and vigorously shook his whole body, getting a good bath. Then after shaking himself somewhat in a similar fashion to a wet dog shaking water off, Ace started on the puddles. Hopping through with both feet, bouncing and sloshing as he goes. *"Splish splash I was takin' a bath."*

The rest of the group were joining in, following right behind him, taking their turns for the deeper part as if waiting in line at a water park, then shaking thoroughly as they come out, some going for seconds.

They were having a really good time at it. I called Chief over and he parked right on the living room window ledge, watching the show with me.

Chase The Ace

September

It had not rained in over a week so things were getting dry. The young ones were in the garden, making raspy caw'nversation. Ace perched in a nearby Maple tree, watching everything I was doing on the balcony.

Gliding down from his branch to the lawn, Ace hopped toward the driveway. The grass and the weeds around the garage were green and tall. The pile of sticks behind the garage must have seemed like a good hiding spot for Hunter, until an overhead crow let out a cry of concern coming from where the driveway meets the garage door, *"SKWAAAAWW!"* -

I looked around, then suddenly I saw Hunter's eyes light up as the angle of the sunlight caught them just for a moment, giving his position away to me. He was in the shadows, past the thick grass behind the garage.

Ace jolted backwards and began flapping his wings, performing an impressive vertical Harrier jet style takeoff, reversing his direction instantly, then flying to the top of the fence, completing his escape with a few choice words for Hunter.

I saw his shadowy figure disappearing back into the long grass around the side of the garage door. Spirit is honking with a few other crows above the garage at the back where the stick pile is. Hunter's in there somewhere beneath the condemning and accusations.

Would Hunter have gone for Ace? Or was he just there for the meat I was tossing for the crows? I didn't think he was there to cause trouble, as he never picked any fights with Chief or the five cats next door. It was just in his curious nature to check everything out.

This was a close call for Ace but he handled it perfectly, and has more than enough backup to ward off an intruder. Encounters like this will add to his confidence, equipping him with a skillset for adventures outside the garden.

The Prince Of Garden Crows

The stars predict his oracle
I've crystal balled his past,
His zodiac's unclear to me
His horoscope comes last,

Fortune is what he seeks
Treasure is what he found,
The shining gifts he brings to us
His DNA is bound,

His future appears uncertain
His history set in stone,
A single shadow in the sun
Yet never seems alone,

Soaring out of somewhere
Rising on the breeze,
Temperature reaches minus
With feet that never freeze,

His attitude's tremendous
With confidence that grows,
A royal and regal specimen
The prince of garden crows.

- Keith Weston

Beyond The Chapters

"Across the observations
And sifting through the notes,
Learning about the life of crows
Around these anecdotes."

A Story Book Ending

Mr. & Mrs. Crow stuck together through their setback, and returned to make a rewarding comeback, contributing their part to the garden. In my eyes, Spirit & Shadow are the King & Queen of the Evergreen Castle, proving they could thrive in this garden, regardless of the weather. That makes Ace the new Prince, and the sky is the limit for him.

What a season to end my stay in this nice location.

Spirit & Shadow, Mr. & Mrs. Crow and their fledglings will get to continue their garden adventure, while a new one begins for Chief and I at my new location near Hammonds Plains.

With the moving date scheduled around the corner of next week, I won't get to follow the fledgling progress anymore. I'll have to say farewell for now to the companions and friends I met here. I will miss this place.

My awareness has changed, from the very first crow that I encountered, his cohorts, the elders, the courtships, the disastrous first spring to the culminating success of the crows in my garden. It has caused me to gain a new level of respect and admiration for all wild creatures roaming our yards.

I am looking forward to meeting some new garden friends …

It was sooner than I expected.

Diet Options

The Crow is a natural scavenger. They will eat almost anything.

This includes a broad range of culinary options from roadkill and insects, to peanuts, berries, and even seeing one fly by with a hamburger clamped in its mouth. This tells me that they're interested in people food just as much as anything else.

If they think they have choice - i.e. I can put fresh bread out and get no response, they will wait for the meat option; *"I know you've got some"* said Mr. Crow with his body language.

They certainly enjoy having access to a fresh water dish to be able to dunk their food in before eating. Often they will dunk the dry foods to help them swallow easier. The mothers will mix the foods throughly with water for easier regurgitation during the process of feeding their young.

Loves:

- Peanuts, in and out of the shell (unsalted*)
- Peanut Butter on Bread
- Hard Boiled Egg Yokes
- Cheese
- Grapes
- Apples/Cores

Also loves most anything meat related, raw or cooked such as:

- Liver, Kidney
- Chicken, Skins
- Ground Beef and Pork
- Beef Fat Trimmings
- Sausages (Mild)

Likes or Will Eat:

- Fish, Cooked and Raw
- Roast Potato
- Pasta
- Banana
- Breads
- Fruit Cake
- Watermelon
- Various Other Nuts
- Oats/Granola
- Sunflower Seeds - Hulled
- Corn - Dried/Cracked, Raw, Cooked
- Some Pet Store Kibble

Dislikes:

- Some Vegetables
- Wet Cat Food
- Citrus, Sour Fruits
- Some Spices
- Some Pasta Sauces

Body Language

Even though I had always tried to keep any movement to a minimum so as not to scare anyone, I began to note that any new crow that landed on the perch wasn't sure what to expect.

When opening the door for the first time to them it was a new experience for both of us. I always opened the kitchen door slowly and quietly, this alone caused any new crow to fly off to a nearby tree.

I began to step out onto the balcony backwards with no eye contact. I did this to indicate to the crow that I wasn't making a fuss about it specifically. This backwards thing introduced a level of comfortability for them.

I made a habit of showing the crow what I was going to give it by holding it out in front of me as I placed it on the perch. No sudden movements. I'd say hello a few times, or make a quiet football rattle sound to greet them.

I found that when I give a strange crow a chunk of fresh beef liver, it notices! They'll give me that look … ***"Wow this is good"***. There's almost a head nod, I've just made a new friend.

I imagine the crow's saying ***"All you have to do is land on the platform and a man will come and put out something nice for you to eat, it's crazy"***.

Crows have a detection process where as soon as you lock eyes with an unfamiliar crow it can become nervous and unsure. Probably wondering why you are staring at it. Until we had gotten to know each other I tried to avoid direct eye contact whenever possible.

Pieces of raw liver were always acceptable under any conditions, but I would never come outside with a pile of scraps and throw them just anywhere. I stayed out and tried feeding who was there. I tried to personalize it for the particular crow in question.

If I threw something on the garage roof I'd wait for the crow or crows to come down to eat it or at least start eating before I came back inside.

For being wild birds I thought that they have dealt with it all very well.

Caws And Effect

I have spent some time listening to the various calls and sounds they make. Far more than just caws, crows appear to have an extended vocabulary full of all different types of sounds from caws to honk, clicks, purrs and rattles.

There's a definite **"Hey, there's food here"**, or **"I'm over here"** call, which sounds like three slow steady caws - **"Caw Caw Caw"**. These caws are usually repeated in sequences of three, but they have various patterns beyonds the triple caw. As witnessed in *'Training Days'* the triple caw is taught by the mother early in the fledglings life.

Another one is the alarm call, quite harsh, coarse, and loud single honks and squawks - multiplied by the number of crows around; often directed right at the cause, usually a cat, blowing its cover.

These short loud alarm honks are a contrasting difference between the softer honks used to get my attention in the kitchen.

When a crow is embarrassed or not happy they can make clicking or ticking noises, as I noted in *'Getting To Know Mr. Crow'* where on one occasion I prevented him from landing on the perch. I didn't realize that I had crossed an imaginary line. Mr. Crow was extremely upset that I had blocked him. Made seemingly worse because we had an audience of his peers looking on. After landing he looked most indignant. Shaking himself continuously and muttering crow insults at me as he adjusted his composure. Uttering a series of quite loud clicks *"TCK TCK TCK!"* accompanied by exaggerated full body flicks as he was explaining to me that I am not allowed to do that again. I agreed.

I had noticed that when a crow lands in a tree very close to another crow, the one in the tree would greet the visitor with a rattling sound. Nothing like a caw or honk, this sound was very similar to a football game rattle.. *"prrt..rrt.rrt..prrt..rrt"*, I think it means *"Hi, it's safe here"*, or something to the equivalent. I began to mimic this rattle sound as best I could as my general hello, when greeting a new crow or sometimes when feeding a nervous crow.

They are capable of a surprising range of tone inflection. If needed they can call in backup with an urgent tone, or call in friends for a perch party with a softer tone. When in groups they can make chattering sounds to each other.

Their intricate long and short range warning systems are a critical factor concerning their continued survival as Corvids.

There are probably various situations where a juvenile has cried *"Wolf"*, which means in essence a false alarm, as it learns about needing help sometimes, and providing it personally when necessary. If a young crow in training accidentally calls out an alarm by an unintentional mistake I assume it will be corrected in the process by the parents so the usage will be more appropriate next time.

In any battle of the skies, after multiple crows have been summoned and achieved their goal, there appears to be a sound used to signal an *"All Clear"*, or *"Clear Out"*, which I also witnessed in *'A Crow Funeral'* after their moment of silence.

The low muffled honk I heard during the 'Garden Courtship' was unlike any of the other sounds they made.

Even with these observations, their language still holds many secrets yet to be discovered.

Crowmunities

A step beyond a single family's nest, I am beginning to see how all of the crows I met here could belong to a larger community. There also appears to be a ranking system amongst the adult crows, as they show reverence for the more senior members. I have seen an arrogant, greedy male literally cower in the presence of what I determined to be another crow of higher stature, I referred to these as Elders in chapter one under *'Meeting The Elders'*. These crows have an almost regal bearing and are very sure of themselves especially when alone.

They all seem to be on the lookout for each other. As mentioned in the *'Watch Tower'*, I've noticed what appear to be crows on watch, sitting in a quiet spot, in a garden or at the side of a road, usually high up on top of a pole. Always ready to alert others of food becoming available, or to the warning of a cat. Without hesitation, a certain call can bring hundreds of crows to assist.

Almost all of the crow to crow interactions I observed were friendly and social in general. Other than the gestures of rank around the perch, I have never seen any fights amongst crows, but they do gang up quite quickly if necessary to help each other out. I have seen them drive a single crow out of their immediate locale, as well as the one situation I noted in *'Historical Hatching'*, where a crow was immediately chased out of my garden, as the crows level of protection heightened during the week of the hatching.

For the most part, they demonstrated a layer of caring for each other I did not expect. At times showing signs of affection as well as sharing with each other or waiting for their mate to begin eating.

Along the way I've had to remind myself that all these crows are wild, yet still behaving with manners and etiquette. My intention was to provide support for the two families of crows; not be their sole source of food. They seemed to know it was special thing to get treats on a landing perch.

They respected each other in and around my garden, behaving with their crowmunity in mind.

From The Author

Greetings, and thank you for reading this book.

I am a retired male, and just happened to be residing at a suitably quiet location frequently visited by several crows.

My only other notable previous experience with crows was when I was birdwatching as a young boy with my cousin in the United Kingdom during our summer holidays.

We saw a crows nest high up in an old dead spindly tall tree next to a secluded pond on the edge of a farm in East Anglia. I climbed up warily to the constant goading from my cousin to go higher. I could barely get up close enough to get my hand inside the nest. I felt a solitary cold egg, which I put in my mouth as I needed both hands to navigate my way back down. During my descent, I slipped, breaking a branch beneath me, while simultaneously breaking the egg in my mouth. The egg was rotten.. and maybe I got my deserving reward.

Acknowledgements

I would like to offer my profound thanks to everyone who has knowingly or unknowingly participated in the creation of this work. From the crows themselves, to the seagulls and starlings, the ospreys, the cats, and my next door neighbour, who had often commented regarding on what she had witnessed first hand.

A special thanks to my son Keith for his dedicated efforts, encouragement and continued support in the completion of the book.

Holiday Crow Party

December

I had recently moved into an established large lotted subdivision near Hammonds Plains, which is a few minutes from Halifax, as the crow flies. Admittedly this is a very quiet place with hardly any traffic other than local inhabitants passing in and out.

On the 24th of December 2016, the eve of our holiday celebrations, at about 3:00 pm, I was arriving home with my son from some last minute shopping and, after turning into the cul-de-sac, it wasn't long before I had to slow right down, we couldn't believe our eyes as we were approaching a complete blanketing, on the ground, of solid crows in every direction. It could only be described as a spectacle.

The temperature was showing approximately 6 degrees Celsius on my car dashboard. The winds were calm; the sky was completely overcast with swirls of darker clouds slowly drifting overhead.

The lots in the sub-division are well treed and in excess of an acre each with fairly large front and back gardens with a mixture of hardwoods, softwoods and decorational plants.

In the road directly in front of us and upon both sides of it, spreading over at least three lots on each side were, hundreds and hundreds of crows. The road and all three lawns on each side were packed with crows, just mulling about. I slowed down and proceeded to crawl along as not to alarm or injure them.

Nothing seemed to faze them at all and they didn't mind moving out of the way. They were obviously in no hurry to leave. We turned into our driveway and beheld the sight. Sitting in the car we saw that there were just as many crows in every possible tree and on every branch. The noise of all these crows calling each other was a little overwhelming. We were absolutely fascinated.

The crows showed no signs of leaving, we were crowstruck. I had never even heard or read of anything like this before. There had to be over 2000 crows. There were hundreds not dozens, on each lawn and as many on the road, one to three feet apart.

I parked the car backwards in the driveway and we watched in awe, admiring this rare event for about another 12 to 15 minutes, taking it all in. My phone was dead. I was unable to get any of this on video. What was going on?

The crows seemed to have decided that this was over and time to get back to normal business. They slowly began to leave, one by one and in groups, they picked up and gradually dissipated in a southwesterly direction.

I saw a neighbour admiring the situation from a couple of lots away so I walked over and asked him what he made of it and, how long he had lived here. His reply was that during 11 years he had never seen anything remotely close to this and had no answer, nor offered any clarification to this occurrence. I questioned another neighbour, a 17 year inhabitant who said a similar story to the first, including his years in rural New Brunswick.

To the best of my knowledge this was in no way anything like the crow funeral I personally witnessed. Perhaps this seemingly well organized gathering was a pre-roost, or maybe as my son and I jokingly referred to it as *"A Holiday Crow Party"*.

P.S. I did receive a Crow Caller under the tree this year. Apparently it makes the sound of a crow calling for backup. I look forward to experimenting with it in the future.

My Notes & Observations

Title: _____

Date: _____

Notes & Observations:

_____
_____
_____
_____
_____
_____
_____
_____
_____
_____
_____
_____
_____
_____
_____
_____
_____
_____

My Notes & Observations

Title: _____

Date: _____

Notes & Observations:

_____
_____
_____
_____
_____
_____
_____
_____
_____
_____
_____
_____
_____
_____
_____
_____

My Notes & Observations

Title: _____

Date: _____

Notes & Observations:

_____

_____

_____

_____

_____

_____

_____

_____

_____

_____

_____

_____

_____

_____

_____

_____

_____

My Notes & Observations

Title: _____

Date: _____

Notes & Observations:

_____

_____

_____

_____

_____

_____

_____

_____

_____

_____

_____

_____

_____

_____

_____

_____

_____

My Notes & Observations

Title: _____

Date: _____

Notes & Observations:

_____

_____

_____

_____

_____

_____

_____

_____

_____

_____

_____

_____

_____

_____

_____

_____

_____

My Notes & Observations

Title: _____

Date: _____

Notes & Observations:

_____

_____

_____

_____

_____

_____

_____

_____

_____

_____

_____

_____

_____

_____

_____

_____

Tell Your Story -

You can send in your own crow stories or poems to:

Email: *thecrowsinmygarden@gmail.com*

Want To Know More?

Visit us at our website for more information:

Website: *thecrowsinmygarden.com*

Printed in Great Britain
by Amazon

42070958R00136